Cambridge Elements

Elements in New Religious Movements
Series Editor
Rebecca Moore
San Diego State University
Founding Editor
†James R. Lewis
Wuhan University

SANTA MUERTE DEVOTION

Vulnerability, Protection, Intimacy

Wil G. Pansters
Utrecht University

Shaftesbury Road, Cambridge CB2 8EA, United Kingdom

One Liberty Plaza, 20th Floor, New York, NY 10006, USA

477 Williamstown Road, Port Melbourne, VIC 3207, Australia

314–321, 3rd Floor, Plot 3, Splendor Forum, Jasola District Centre, New Delhi – 110025, India

103 Penang Road, #05–06/07, Visioncrest Commercial, Singapore 238467

Cambridge University Press is part of Cambridge University Press & Assessment, a department of the University of Cambridge.

We share the University's mission to contribute to society through the pursuit of education, learning and research at the highest international levels of excellence.

www.cambridge.org
Information on this title: www.cambridge.org/9781009619707

DOI: 10.1017/9781009446631

© Wil G. Pansters 2025

This publication is in copyright. Subject to statutory exception and to the provisions of relevant collective licensing agreements, no reproduction of any part may take place without the written permission of Cambridge University Press & Assessment.

When citing this work, please include a reference to the DOI 10.1017/9781009446631

First published 2025

A catalogue record for this publication is available from the British Library

ISBN 978-1-009-61970-7 Hardback
ISBN 978-1-009-44661-7 Paperback
ISSN 2635-232X (online)
ISSN 2635-2311 (print)

Cambridge University Press & Assessment has no responsibility for the persistence or accuracy of URLs for external or third-party internet websites referred to in this publication and does not guarantee that any content on such websites is, or will remain, accurate or appropriate.

Santa Muerte Devotion

Vulnerability, Protection, Intimacy

Elements in New Religious Movements

DOI: 10.1017/9781009446631
First published online: February 2025

Wil G. Pansters
Utrecht University
Author for correspondence: Wil G. Pansters, w.g.pansters@uu.nl

Abstract: In recent decades, the cult of Santa Muerte has become a remarkable phenomenon in Mexico's popular religious landscape, from where it has migrated abroad. Due to the uncommon iconography of the robed skeleton and the association with criminality, the Santa Muerte cult has been the object of public controversy. This Element deconstructs mainstream views of Santa Muerte devotion by privileging the voices and practices of devotees. Counterintuitively, Santa Muerte devotion is about assuring a good life in health, work, love, justice, and security. Notwithstanding the cult's rapid growth and public visibility since 2000, it is deeply embedded in Mexico's religious and cultural history. The analysis of material culture, theology, and ritual demonstrates the importance of devotional intimacy. This Element also studies how gender, family, leadership, and political relations intersect with the cult. Santa Muerte popular religiosity is examined in terms of socio-economic vulnerabilities, ineffective social protections, exclusion, and existential insecurities.

Keywords: Santa Muerte, popular religion, ritual, vulnerability, Catholicism

© Wil G. Pansters 2025

ISBNs: 9781009619707 (HB), 9781009446617 (PB), 9781009446631 (OC)
ISSNs: 2635-232X (online), 2635-2311 (print)

Contents

	Introduction	1
1	Origins and Background of Santa Muerte Devotion	9
2	Material Culture and Spaces of Santa Muerte Devotion	21
3	Ritual and Theology of Santa Muerte Devotion	35
4	The Organization and Politics of Santa Muerte Devotion	49
5	Santa Muerte Devotion and Society: Vulnerability, Insecurity, and the Roman Catholic Church	58
	Epilogue	68
	References	72

Introduction

From the city of San Luis Potosí, we headed north on federal Highway 57, a key artery that connects Mexico City with major northeastern industrial cities all the way to Piedras Negras on the Mexico–US border. After approximately 100 kilometres, my friend and I arrived at the junction with Highway 80, which runs eastwards towards the Gulf of Mexico. Popularly known as El Huizache, the junction is a typical highway microcosm on northern Mexico's desertic highlands that caters to a fleeting population. With a gas station, car repair shops, restaurants, and a few grocery stores, it is a place where travellers take a break from their long drives. For years, this part of the highway has attracted criminals involved in carjacking and cargo theft. Coming from southern Mexico and the Pacific coast, drugs pass through here on their way to US consumers. El Huizache has a reputation of being unsafe. Although in 2021 a detachment of the National Guard was stationed here, many travellers feel they need additional protection.

In the surroundings of the junction, one finds three Santa Muerte – Saint Death – shrines. One is small and scruffy with dried up flowers and bird droppings. Another is a small-scale rectangular green structure with bright red inner walls. A well-kept narrow corridor has burning candles, paper flowers, Santa Muerte posters, and a niche with four effigies of the saint. On the western side of Highway 57, the third shrine is a maroon 'capilla de la santa-muerte' [*sic*]. Concrete steps lead towards an open, white-painted cast iron gate. With its 4-by-6 metre surface and approximately 3.5 metres height, this is an impressive shrine. It is about fifteen metres from the main road. Day and night cars and trucks whiz by at high speed. It is noisy and dusty. Every so often, cars and trucks stop. Visitors make their way to the shrine, usually after buying a candle or something else in the adjoining shop-restaurant. At one point, a middle-aged man parks his automobile near the shrine. Dressed in shorts and a T-shirt, sporting tattooed arms and legs, the man kneels in front of the altar and prays silently. Shortly afterwards, a young woman and her daughter visit the chapel. The daughter leaves some coins. And so it goes on.

Two prayer stools face the main altar, which consists of a stepped platform that has a massive seated black skeletal Santa Muerte statue at the centre. She holds a globe in her left hand and a scythe in her right hand. The lower steps hold numerous different-sized effigies all dressed in cloth habits. Together they form an extraordinarily colourful bunch. Offerings like candles and flowers fill the lowest step. A large arch of pink and purple crepe paper encircles the entirety. Large windows and a dome in the ceiling emphasize the shrine's unusual spaciousness (Figure 1).

Figure 1 Altar in Capilla de la Santa Muerte, El Huizache junction, San Luis Potosí. Photo by author.

Several human-sized dressed statues line the yellow inner walls, which are covered with large, framed Santa Muerte posters. Some have photographs stuck on them of the devotees requesting Santa Muerte's protection. Unsurprisingly, quite a few are truck drivers, who spend weeks on the road away from loved ones, living on junk food and pills, risking accidents, robberies, or worse. A spectacular example of a tailor-made poster contains a Santa Muerte image on top of which a cut-out photograph of a chauffeur in front of his double truck is glued. The skeletal saint wears a white robe, her grisly skull, surrounded by an aureole, looks down on the driver. Underneath the image is a prayer. The poster's skillful composition conveys both an intimidating threat and an overpowering source of protection (Figure 2).

Elsewhere in the shrine is a wooden display case full of small passport pictures and IDs, and photographs of more truck drivers, couples, families, and children. At the bottom of the display case are some Santa Muerte figurines, and a replica skull open at the top, in which someone has put out a cigarette.

Figure 2 Santa Muerte poster, Capilla de la Santa Muerte, El Huizache junction, San Luis Potosí. Photo by author.

Only twenty-five years ago it would have been highly unlikely to encounter such a public shrine dedicated to Santa Muerte. Today, a neat signpost on Highway 57 informs travellers of the approaching shrine. Altars and shrines can be found across the country and beyond. A wide variety of devotional accoutrements – figurines, lotions, bracelets – are for sale in popular markets, where people buy vegetables, meat, get haircuts, eat lunch, and find products for their physical and spiritual well-being. Devotees gather at street rosaries (devotional rituals), processions, and pilgrimages, and are active on social media. In other words, over a relatively brief period Santa Muerte iconography and devotion gained a visible presence in Mexico's religious and cultural landscape.

Santa Muerte devotion has been around since before 2000, but without its current public exposure and with different devotional practices. Compared to its current exuberance, during most of the twentieth century the cult existed in an elementary form, above all concealed in private spaces. It therefore seems justifiable to speak of a new religious movement, even though it is more a broad, diverse, and changing community of congregations than a single movement. This does not mean it lacks significant social and political components. Devotees and scholars alike frequently use the nomenclature of cult ('culto' in Spanish) rather than church, community, or, much less, movement. I use the word cult in a descriptive sense as 'a community loosely cohered by belief in a particular folk saint', which avoids the negative common usage of the term in English, for which Spanish speakers would rather use the term 'secta' (Graziano 2007: ix). While relatively new in its current form, and less a movement than a cult, the Santa Muerte phenomenon is unquestionably religious: devotees speak of their beliefs, altars, rituals, and their allegiance to the saint (and God) with passion and faith. In general, I understand the cult as an idiosyncratic yet deeply embedded manifestation of Mexican repertoires of popular religiosity.

For many, however, this is implausible: the cult's uncommon fearsome skeletal iconography is seen as antithetical to mainstream religious experiences. Over the years, I have observed a range of attitudes towards the cult and my research: from raising eyebrows, disbelief, and warnings not to get into trouble to the outright condemnation of the cult as delusion, idolatry, and satanism. The cult's increasing public presence should therefore not be taken as an unequivocal sign of normalization. Although attitudes have shifted, it remains controversial and stigmatized. The Catholic Church has characterized it as a dangerous aberration. Since the beginning of the twenty-first century, the increasingly visible manifestations of Santa Muerte devotion attracted the attention of the mainstream media. Especially during the first decade of the 2000s, documentaries and journalistic accounts portrayed the cult and its members as associated with crime, drug trafficking, and violence. Hollywood movies and series soon picked up on the trope. On Santa Muerte social media pages people leave messages of hell and damnation.

In this Element, I propose to deconstruct mainstream views of Santa Muerte devotion by privileging the voices, experiences, and practices of devotees themselves that continue to be only superficially known. I argue that, counterintuitively but quintessentially, Santa Muerte devotion is about securing a good life. I will show how despite its distinctive features it is profoundly shaped by Mexico's religious and cultural history. Santa Muerte material culture, theology, and devotional practices echo rituals performed for canonized Catholic saints, including the Virgin of Guadalupe. Based on first-hand ethnographical fieldwork conducted since 2014, as well as an in-depth examination of existing scholarly work, this Element presents a comprehensive overview and analysis of Santa Muerte devotion. While it can be found in the United States and elsewhere, the focus of this Element is on Santa Muerte devotion in Mexico.

Background and Context

Since the early 2000s, the cult has become more visible, grown numerically, and expanded geographically. Assessing the number of devotees is notably difficult. The cult has no membership registration or entry requirements. While most scholars have accepted that reliable quantitative data about the cult are unavailable, others have resorted to disputable indicators of interested cult leaders to gauge the number of devotees. In 2012, extrapolating from the estimated sales of votive candles and other devotional accoutrements – a statistically hazardous task – the religion scholar Andrew Chesnut calculated the number of Santa Muerte devotees at five million (2012: 8–9). Only a few years later, in 2015, the cult had grown 'astronomically' arriving at ten to twelve million devotees in Mexico, Central America, and the United States (McNearney 2015). Adrián Yllescas (2023: 188) has concluded that these claims lack methodological rigor, and instead pointed at anthropologist Regnar Kristensen's (2015) painstaking 2008 census of Mexico City street altars that arrived at approximately 30,000 devotees praying monthly at public shrines. Assuming that this represents one-third of all devotees in the city – many only worship in their homes or in prison – and that the number of devotees has doubled in ten years (as Chesnut suggests), we arrive at around 200,000 in the Mexico City metropolitan area around 2018. Since nearly one-fifth of the country's population lives in the greater Mexico City area – the cult's heartland – it seems reasonable to estimate the total number of devotees at one million in Mexico at the time. While it has been argued that the number of devotees at public gatherings was decreasing by the end of the 2010s, a possible post-Covid rise would currently render at most 1.25 million devotees (Kristensen 2019: 151).

There is compelling evidence of the cult's internationalization. Research has documented altars and congregations from Los Angeles to New York (Graf 2023; Jiménez 2019; Müller 2021). As in Mexico, reliable statistics don't exist. However, ethnographic research provides useful clues, particularly about Los Angeles, arguably the most important centre of Santa Muerte devotion outside Mexico (Graf 2023: 28). It has shown that compared to Mexico numbers are very modest. While the busiest shrine in Los Angeles is visited on workdays by devotees for individual prayers, services provided on Sundays attracted around 25 participants, and around 100 attended the most important annual fiesta (Graf 2023: 91). Another shrine offers weekend services for 5–20 people, and another has a successful digital platform with 80,000 members, of which more than 80 per cent are based in Mexico, with only 179 members hailing from Los Angeles itself (Jiménez 2019: 147–8). In 2015, the main annual festivity of New York's most important shrine attracted around 300 devotees (Higuera Bonfil 2016: 244). A generous extrapolation from national hot spots renders no more than a few hundred thousand devotees in the United States and Canada. Considering Central America's entire population of 53 million (2023), it seems reasonable to add another few hundred thousand devotees, making a current total of 1.5–2 million devotees – an impressive number for a cult practically unknown twenty-five years ago.[1]

Understanding the evolution of Santa Muerte devotion warrants a look at the main shifts in Mexico's religious landscape. First, during the last half a century Mexico experienced a sustained trend towards religious diversity. Whereas in 1950 around 98 per cent of the population defined as Catholic, by 2000 this was 87 per cent, a significant decline but less markedly than in the rest of Latin America (Blancarte 2005: 225; Ramírez 2009: 80). By 2020, the percentage had further dropped to 77 per cent. The largest part of the population no longer adhering to Catholicism belongs to an array of evangelical and biblical denominations (about 12 per cent), while the rest is made up of other religious currents, and the nebulous but large group of three million people (about 2.5 per cent) categorized as 'believers without religious affiliation' (INEGI 2021).

Second, there has been the profound impact of secularization, which comprises not only 9.5 million people with no religion in 2020 (ca. 7.5 per cent) but also the significant development, especially among Catholics, of more freedom of conscience in moral and religious matters. Without breaking with their faith, Catholic believers increasingly regulate their lives at a distance from the

---

[1] There is no evidence that devotees in other parts of the world exceed 10,000–20,000.

ecclesiastic normativity and eliminate 'institutional intermediaries in the search of salvation' (Blancarte 2005: 227).

Third, a key feature of Mexico's changing religious landscape concerns the meanings and practices of popular Catholicism. There is evidence of a 'loosening' creed: 47 per cent and 18 per cent of Catholics identified as 'traditional' and 'sui generis' believers, respectively, as opposed to a quarter as believers 'by conviction' (ENCREER 2016: 33).[2] Thus, for two-thirds of Mexican Catholics denominational identity has more to do with culturally inherited religious rituals than with underlying ecclesiastically sanctioned beliefs and norms. Being a 'sui generis' Catholic connotes a 'remarkable permeability to heterodox beliefs and practices' (ENCREER 2016: 62). In fact, most Santa Muerte devotees continue to think of themselves as Catholics. Since the 1960s, Mexican Catholics have 'completed an enormous *silent revolution* through which they have, stealthily and slowly, become independent from the hierarchical dominance [of the Church] over their daily actions' (Blancarte 2005: 297).

Finally, sociocultural trends and political conditions during the late 1980s led to constitutional reforms in religious matters. Ever since the Mexican revolution (1910–1917), the state had not recognized the legal status of churches and religious associations. The 1992 constitutional reform normalized relations by granting all existing churches juridical status as religious associations and citizens the right to establish new ones. It also allowed them buying and selling real estate properties. Voting rights of the clergy were restored (Blancarte 2005: 285–7; Ramírez 2009: 66–7).

The expansion and changing face of Santa Muerte devotion in the early twenty-first century soon drew scholarly attention. This was partly a response to journalistic reports and literary accounts (Ambrosio 2003; Aridjis 2003). According to Spanish anthropologist Juan Antonio Flores Martos, these were fraught with a 'superficial, sensationalistic vision for [popular] dissemination that explored – and exploited – this cult' (2007: 281). Mexican anthropologist Perla Fragoso commented that they associated Santa Muerte devotion with illegality and crime (2007b: 24). Both called for serious scholarly research. Leaving aside scattered references by previous generations of anthropologists (see Section 1), at the time of this call a few scholarly texts had already been published. As a religious phenomenon in the making, Santa Muerte constituted a fascinating laboratory and sparked a new research field. By the early 2000s, a pattern in reporting and studying the cult was already discernible.

---

[2] Here 'sui generis' refers to 'in their own way' ('a su manera' in Spanish), rather than following ecclesiastic prescriptions.

First, journalistic interest in the cult has remained strong in Mexico and abroad (Gil Olmos 2010; Lorusso 2013). This includes reports in newspapers, magazines, and books, but also documentaries, films, and blogs. This interest cannot be dissociated from brutal drug trafficking-related violence and militarized government responses. Second, Elsa Malvido's seminal 2005 article about the cult's iconographic and religious precedents inaugurated the first wave of studies from Mexican anthropology. Katia Perdigón published the first book about Santa Muerte (2008), while Fragoso's 2007 Master Thesis started an unabated stream of postgraduate anthropological dissertations. Theirs and the later work of De la Fuente, García Zavala, Garcés Marrero, Hernández Hernández, Higuera Bonfil, Valverde Montaño, Yllescas Illescas, and others represent essential contributions to understanding Santa Muerte devotion. Third, John Thompson and Claudio Lomnitz's early work marked the beginning of a significant involvement of US and especially European (anthropological) scholarship. The latter included the work of Argyriadis, Bigliardi, Flores Martos, Graf, Huffschmid, Kristensen, Lamrani, Mancini, Michalik, Müller, and Perrée, while the former included that of Roush, Kingsbury, and Chesnut, who published the first English-language book on the cult.

This Element draws upon my own ethnographic research carried out since 2014, as well as the scholarship by this ever more integrated network of researchers, the quantity and quality of which debunks Malgorzata Oleszkiewicz-Peralba's unwarranted assertion that 'there is almost no scholarly literature' on Santa Muerte (2015: 104). With its global expansion, the study of the cult has matured and moved in different conceptual, methodological, and thematic directions. At least three shifts can be identified. First, alongside the study of origins, iconography, and societal context, a new interest in the experiences and daily practices of devotees has arisen, using concepts as lived religion (Garcés Marrero 2021; Yllescas Illescas 2023) and *poiēsis* (Graf 2023). In this Element, I use the term 'religion-making' and stress the importance of bottom-up agency. Second, while early publications largely focused on devotional centres and practices in Mexico City, more and more research has been carried out elsewhere in Mexico and beyond. This Element draws on my fieldwork at different congregations not only in the capital but also in San Luis Potosí, Guadalajara, Puebla, and Ciudad Juárez. Finally, thematic and conceptual diversification has produced comparative work about music, attire, tattoos, gender, migration, and articulations with other popular religions. Since the cult of Saint Death is alive and well, much empirical and interpretative research lies ahead.

Section 1 examines the origins of Santa Muerte devotion and popular narratives about them. I discuss the histories of specific (Catholic) religious practices and iconographies as well as Mexican traditions of mortuary imagery. Acknowledging ethnographical, historiographical, and archival limitations, I argue that historically distinctive features of popular Latin American Catholicism compose the quintessential 'mold' of current Santa Muerte devotion, with its visual exuberance, expressive creativity, and symbolic enjoyment. Section 2 reviews the material culture and expressive forms of the cult and considers how these relate to the 'personification' and intimacy of the saint. It also examines key places of worship. I argue that the vibrancy and expressive diversity of Santa Muerte material culture is driven by grassroots devotional agency. Section 3 studies devotional practices and rituals such as individual prayers and offerings, and collective gatherings. At the core of Santa Muerte beliefs and theology lie unconditional faith and reciprocity centred on acquiring protection and support. Expressive diversity, the absence of a sanctioned canon, popular religion-making, and devotional and ritualistic agency both enable and are shaped by the cult's organizational and political structures and dynamics, which is the subject of Section 4. Section 5 focuses on the social and economic contextualization of Santa Muerte practices. I investigate vulnerable livelihoods, ineffective social protections, and insecurity, which constitute a breeding ground for ordinary citizens to look for protection from alternative transcendental entities. The impact of the COVID-19 pandemic is briefly examined. This section ends with a look at the cult's relationship with the Catholic Church. An Epilogue closes this Element.

1 Origins and Background of Santa Muerte Devotion

For most people the first encounter with a Santa Muerte effigy produces feelings of bewilderment, disquiet or even indignation. And yet, Santa Muerte popular religiosity is far from an extraneous element in Mexico's sociocultural landscape but part of its rich religious tapestries. For centuries social groups and institutions with dissimilar ideas about faith and spirituality were involved in weaving and undoing these tapestries. To explore these complex processes, this section first distinguishes between popular (emic) narratives about Santa Muerte's origins and scholarly (etic) work. Shifting to the latter, the analysis differentiates between histories of specific popular religious iconographies and practices, and broader symbolic repertoires about death and the dead. The former surveys skeletal images and imageries in colonial Mexico, with a brief excursion into precolonial imaginations of death as well as the rich history of Catholic folk saints, shrines, and miraculous images. The latter looks at broad cultural traditions of mortuary imagery, especially as represented by the Day of the Dead celebrations, and the secular imagery of the dressed female skeleton known as the Catrina. Subsequently this section reviews ethnographical findings of embryonic Santa Muerte devotion. The section concludes that these interrelated historical resources and cultural repertoires are all relevant for understanding the present-day Santa Muerte cult, but also that evidence to sustain the cult's uninterrupted historical existence since precolonial times is tenuous.

Popular Narratives of Santa Muerte Origins

During a visit to the República market in San Luis Potosí I meet Saúl. He runs an esoteric stall, where he does cleansings and Tarot card readings. The most eye-catching object at the stall is a large Santa Muerte effigy in a red gown, a white skull with a black wig and a crown; in her right hand she holds a globe topped by another skull. Somebody put a white rose in her left hand. A jack of all religious trades, Saúl sees himself as a 'gypsy, santero and spiritist'. He doesn't doubt that Santa Muerte has pre-Hispanic origins. Rooted in Aztec cosmology, the current cult is directly related to Mictlantecuhtli – lord of the underworld. During Spanish colonial rule the cult was forced to go underground, literally. Saúl explains that underneath the Tepito neighbourhood in downtown Mexico City a network of catacombs exists, where the warrior–deity Mictlantecuhtli was venerated. Once a year, at the beginning of November, devotees would secretly enter the catacombs and perform rituals. In his view, these colonial rituals are forerunners of current devotional practices. Situating the origins of Santa Muerte in a clandestine Aztec death cult, this emic narrative can be read as a metaphor for a concealed precolonial indigenous religion that lies beneath Mexican Catholicism, constituting the essence of Mexican national identity and religiosity. For Saúl, today's Day of the Dead rituals are a continuation of the Aztec cult and a form of Santa Muerte devotion.[3]

Another common emic narrative situates the origins of Santa Muerte devotion in the mid-nineteenth century, when the saint appeared to a shaman or witch (*brujo*) in the coastal state of Veracruz. In the dream, the saint charged him to disseminate the cult since Mexico was to be her homeland. The cult's first devotees are therefore believed to come from Veracruz, which occupies a prominent place in Mexico's spiritual and religious landscape (Olavarrieta Marenco 1977; Papenfuss 2023). In this narrative, the roots of Santa Muerte devotion are also related to postcolonial indigenous knowledge and beliefs. Unsurprisingly, narrative variations exist. Some claim the first image of Santa Muerte appeared at the end of the eighteenth century in Sombrerete in the

---

[3] Except for nationally known cult leaders, this study uses pseudonyms of informants' first names. Interview with Saúl, San Luis Potosí, 15 July 2022.

northern state of Zacatecas, where she was worshipped by miners. In yet another emic narrative a local shrine owner claimed indigenous Purépecha roots in the western state of Michoacán going back to the sixteenth century (Chesnut 2012: 28–9).

Alternatively, another current within the Santa Muerte community maintains that it was the arrival of the Spanish that set off the cult. Catholic missionaries used European narratives, songs, and artistic representations of death in their evangelization work. These were subsequently captured in paintings, murals, and effigies in the churches and convents of New Spain.

Today, these emic narratives and innumerable variations about the pre-Hispanic, indigenist, syncretic, or Catholic origins of Santa Muerte devotion circulate in the tales of congregational leaders and ordinary devotees, booklets, magazines, documentaries, and websites. The absence of a canon creates space for popular religion-making, which bestows legitimacy upon people's beliefs by anchoring them in the nation's deep historical past. The key significance of emic narratives is that constructing foundational Santa Muerte mythologies and devotional practices largely lies in the hands of diverse congregations, leaders, and individual devotees. Adhering to one or another narrative shapes prayers, rituals, and artefacts.

Iconographic Echoes from the Past

Since the start of the twenty-first century, the swelling number of Santa Muerte devotees and the cult's increased public visibility sparked popular and scholarly interest in its origins. The first scholarly wave was particularly drawn to researching its historical roots and tracing iconographies and devotional practices that resemble today's cult.

From late medieval European Catholicism, images of the Triumph of Death arrived in the New World, mostly in the form of wooden skeletal-crowned figures. Often fixed to a simple cart, they would be taken out for funerary rituals or Holy Week processions to remind people of life's fragility and futility. As religious orders mobilized the effigies' symbolic potency for evangelization, indigenous devotees adopted them in ways that frequently transgressed ecclesiastical boundaries, triggering a dynamic of syncretism, censorship, resistance, prohibition, and popular appropriation that has continued until today. A few of these wooden skeletal sculptures have survived as saints. During the second half of the twentieth century, or even before, most of these saints were seen as precursors of Santa Muerte devotion. Well-known examples are San Pascualito in Chiapas, San Bernardo in Hidalgo, and Nuestra Señora, La Muerte from Yanhuitlán (aka La Santa Muerte de Yanhuitlán), nowadays a small originally

Mixtec village in Oaxaca with an impressive former Dominican convent and church (Perdigón 2008: 121–9; Valverde 2018: 66–92).

The case of San Pascualito is particularly significant. Pascual Bailón was a sixteenth-century Franciscan monk (1540–92), beatified in 1618 and canonized in 1690. His figure was originally popularized by Franciscan friars in current Guatemala and the Mexican state of Chiapas. During the 1650 pest epidemic, a skeletal San Pascualito appeared to a moribund Kaqchikel Indian, offering salvation from the pestilence in exchange for making him the patron saint of the Indians (Navarrete 1982). The indigenous population adopted and reconfigured San Pascualito as a skeleton saint to their needs (Rodríguez López 2022: 96–130). At a time when Catholic officialdom became increasingly concerned about properly distinguishing between legitimate and illegitimate access to supernatural power, the clerical authorities soon viewed San Pascualito devotion as ignorance and religious corruption (Smith 2008: 23). The church issued orders that all statues be collected from the Indians and burned publicly (Navarrete 1982: 30). Yet these efforts were unable to eliminate the ambivalence of the religious colonial order in which indigenous devotees consistently contested institutional regulations.

As accommodation prevailed over polarization, the cult of San Pascualito found its place within the church. The skeletal image resurfaced in a late-nineteenth-century document (1872) about a confraternity placing an image of the skeleton in a coffin in a church in Tuxtla Gutiérrez. New anthropological work has examined how this saint became associated with diverse religious configurations, including Santa Muerte (Rodríguez López 2022). Nowadays, in a reverse movement, Santa Muerte devotees consider San Pascualito as one of the cult's precursors and hold pilgrimages (Valverde 2018: 80).

Despite San Pascualito's documentary trail, scholars have noted with good reason that the historiographic gap between the mid-seventeenth century and the second half of the nineteenth century is so large that claiming historical continuity requires further research (Navarrete 1982: 35; Rodríguez López 2022). This caveat, however, does not question the family resemblance between San Pascualito – and the other saints mentioned – and Santa Muerte iconography. Nor does it invalidate emic narratives about the cult's origins. For anthropologist Lomnitz 'it seems entirely possible that the cult of La Santísima Muerte ... is indeed an evolution of this cult [of San Pascualito]' (2005: 489).

While the San Pascualito case is well documented, there are some additional sources, especially from the eighteenth century, referring to images of death worshipped by indigenous folk, sometimes referred to as Santa Muerte. A 1793 inquisitorial report refers to an idol called 'justo juez' [rightful judge] in the form of a crowned skeleton carrying a bow and arrow (Perdigón 2008: 31–3).[4] In 1797, in San Luis de la Paz, an Indian confraternity organized nightly processions to worship 'Santa Muerte' (Gruzinski 1990: 219). The church resolved to destroy the 'pagan' chapel. At the same time, Catholic discourse employed the image of a skeleton (death) for its own purposes. A fascinating example is the late eighteenth-century publication in Mexico City of *La Portentosa Vida de la Muerte* ('The Prodigious Life of Death') by Franciscan friar Joaquin Bolaños (1792), a work of moralizing fiction that aims 'to induce the fear of death so that the population follows Catholic precepts' (Serna Arnaiz 2017: 133).

If in colonial New Spain popular religious imaginations of death were often framed as having indigenous and pagan origins, Bolaños's book, San Pascual Bailón's case, and the proliferation of images of death in Catholic visual discourse have abundant precedents in medieval Europe, where the Black Death had devastated societies and sparked fears about the fragility of life and the inevitability of (painful) death. New discourses developed within the religious arts, such as the so-called danse macabre, in which skeletons hold the hands of living humans, young and old, rich and poor: death as the great equalizer. The plagues yielded a deep sense of precarious terrestrial and carnal existence and of the sovereign power of death – often portrayed as a crowned skeleton. The church urged people to live a 'good' Christian life, which, in turn, prepared for a 'good' or 'holy' death, '*buena*' or '*santa muerte*'. Treatises laid out how to prepare well for dying (*ars moriendi*).

Discourses and iconographies of death and dying travelled from Europe to the New World. In Mexico, people with the necessary means organized in sodalities that provided members with the services and prayers to assure them a 'buena muerte' (Malvido 2005: 21). Skulls and skeletons became objects of veneration and cults. Doctrinal framing by the church was shaped by indigenous devotees, who built relationships of intimacy with them. Despite occasional persecutions, images of death were 'present, constant, and massive' in colonial Mexico (Perdigón 2008: 29). Lomnitz talks about the 'explosion of death imagery in the public sphere' (2005: 263).

Conversations with Mesoamerican Images of Death

In the New World, discourses and images of death and dying evolved amidst enormous postconquest mortality and entered (hidden) conversations with preHispanic ideas and icons of death. This is a complex matter that requires some

---

[4] In today's cult, Santa Muerte is frequently worshipped as 'justo juez'. There is also a Catholic representation of Christ as 'justo juez'.

contextualization of pre-Hispanic or Mesoamerican ideas and representations of death. Given that connections between contemporary Santa Muerte devotion and pre-Hispanic belief systems are actively assembled by certain cult members as well as assumed by non-specialized observers, a few comments are in place. To start with, the absence of a shared Mesoamerican doctrine and iconography about death warrants precaution: significant variations existed between and within indigenous groups such as the Mexica (or Aztecs), Zapotecs, or Maya. And yet, scholars have ascertained some Mesoamerican commonalities that permit cautiously extrapolating one group's cultural-religious features and placing them in the context of the Spanish Christian other.

Even if some broad similarities between Mesoamerican and Iberian worldviews can be discerned (e.g. the soul outliving the body, topographies of the afterlife), these are overshadowed by profoundly different cosmologies and theologies (Lomnitz 2005: 159). A first key difference concerns the relationship between life and death, and specifically between body and soul. Whereas in the Christian tradition separation of the soul meant the death of the body and eternal reward or punishment for the soul in the hereafter, Mesoamericans understood the relationship as unstable, variable, and, ultimately, multidirectional. The soul or fragments of it could migrate to other species or objects. The living could interact with the souls of the deceased through rituals.

Second, in contrast to the unitary notion of one soul, the Mexica acknowledged the existence of three souls or animating principles (*teyolia*, *tonalli*, *ihiyotl*), each associated with different components of the living body. Depending on how people died, souls travelled in different directions and towards diverse afterlives, one of them being Mictlán, guarded by the male deity Mictlantecuhtli and the female Mictlancíhuatl (often mentioned by Santa Muerte devotees). The Mexica belief that the souls (or spirits) of the dead could inhabit humans was anathema to the Spaniards (Lomnitz 2005: 161–2).

Third, 'the fundamental concept to understand the Mesoamerican peoples is the duality of life and death', involving the core idea that death conserves vital force, that it is a second birth (Matos Moctezuma 2010: 64). One cannot exist without the other, but in a cyclical sense: death as 'the moment of transferal of a life force' (Lomnitz 2005: 166). Hence, Mesoamericans did not understand the afterlife as a space for the final reckoning, but as a transitional and transformative stage towards new life. Finally, the notion of a generative life–death duality expressed itself in distinctive Mesoamerican iconographies, mythologies, and architecture, ranging from early figurines with incarnate and discarnate halves to the anthropogenic Mexica mythology about 'the birth of life and death, united through a constant cycle ... forming a duality' (Matos Moctezuma 2022: 19–62, quotation 61). While for Spaniards skulls symbolized the brevity and vanity of human existence, for Mesoamericans skulls and skeletons were signs 'of earthly rebirth as much as death' because they contained the vestiges of *teyolia* ready to be conveyed to other entities (Lomnitz 2005: 166).

In view of the distinctive attributes of Mesoamerican cosmologies it is not surprising that many scholars have concluded that the current Santa Muerte cult has not evolved from pre-Hispanic civilizations, but that its 'origin is undeniably occidental' (Malvido 2005: 20). Those familiar with Mexica reliefs or effigies related to sacrifice, death, or Mictlántecuhtli would find it difficult to recognize in them iconographic elements of current Santa Muerte images. At the same time, that doesn't exclude the influence wielded by indigenous beliefs and practices on shaping Mexican society and culture during the five centuries since conquest, in particular on the evolution of religious practices that since the sixteenth century had become a key domain of syncretism (Taylor 1996: 51–61). In this context, Roberto Garcés Marrero has suggested that the Santa Muerte cult emerged from the articulation of colonial indigenous beliefs and practices with Catholic notions, which eventually arrived in Mexico City with massive mid-twentieth-century rural–urban migration (2021: 276). It is interesting that the extraordinary iconographic resourcefulness of the current Santa Muerte cult has resulted in 'Aztec' Santa Muerte effigies with feathers and images of the plumed serpent, that certain cult leaders dress up in similar ways, and that some rituals incorporate allegedly pre-Hispanic elements (e.g. dances). These developments seem above all a tribute to Mexico's pre-Hispanic civilizations and an expression of national pride and identity. In that sense, I would hypothesize a popular nationalist dimension of Santa Muerte devotion, a claim to be part of 'Mexicanness'.

The Catholic Devotional Mold

If the Santa Muerte cult feeds upon images from Mexico's religious past, its devotional formats and practices resonate with the overarching religious and cultural Catholic macrosystem (Valverde 2018; see Section 3). Evidence about the origins of Santa Muerte devotion points towards a Catholic cultural template. These historical and cultural connections are non-linear, the result of entangled layers and trajectories of beliefs, iconographies, and rituals. This can above all be observed through the focus on ordinary people's devotional beliefs and practices.

Historian Jennifer Scheper Hughes (2016) succinctly examined the specificities of contemporary popular Catholicism in Latin America. The first springs from the historical circumstances that brought together the colonial imposition of Catholicism by missionaries and the introduction of vernacular Catholic practices and objects by ordinary Spanish settlers in a sociocultural context that featured the engagement of indigenous populations and African slaves and their religious traditions. During the early part of the colonial era, the latter faced economic uncertainty and catastrophic cycles of disease and epidemic (Ramos 2016). Facing existential challenges, indigenous Christians negotiated, resisted, and transformed the institutional European Catholicism. The sustained interactions between different colonial populations meant that 'Latin American Catholicism has drawn on or preserved indigenous or African cultural traditions, incorporating them into new hybrid expressions' (Hughes 2016: 482).

A related feature concerns how the dynamic of imposition, contestation, and accommodation established a pattern in which popular groups historically sought to exert control over the local institutions and religious practices. This generated ambivalent, strained, sometimes hostile relations between popular religious practices (saints, rituals) and ecclesial authorities. Since colonial times de facto popular Catholic canonizations of saints and rituals have been denounced by representatives of orthodoxy as idolatrous.

Another feature of popular Catholicism concerns its entrenched and omnipresent votive culture. The early phase of Spanish colonial rule had coincided with the Catholic Counter-Reformation and the Council of Trent that saw saints as essential for accessing heavenly powers. In the New World's emerging societies, the Crown and Rome's sponsorship of saints encountered a fertile environment: while they played a fundamental role in evangelization, and established cultural bridges between the American colonies and Europe, devotees called upon them to remedy everyday problems and overcome major calamities; they were also instrumental in forging new corporate and political communities, ranging from neighbourhood saints and urban patrons to proto-national religious icons as the Virgin of Guadalupe (Ramos 2016). Votive culture essentially involves ritualized interactions between devotees and saints in fulfillment of a vow (*manda*) through offerings. Offerings may hugely vary, but at its core votive ritual connects devotees to the sacred and to their peers. In Latin American popular Catholicism, the relational element of votive religion is performed in particularly affective, expressive, and imaginative ways. Moreover, votive culture involves mutually caring and intimate relationships between devotees, divine entities, and saints, in which the latter acquire 'their complex status as both material objects and living entities in a way that is uniquely Latin American' and in which a sacred effigy is not only a symbolic representation, but also 'an agentic, animated being: a fully materialized spirit' (Hughes 2016: 484).

Agent 007 and Mexican Mortuary Imageries

The opening scene of the James Bond film *Spectre* (2015) was spectacular. Situated in Mexico City's iconic centre, Secret Agent 007 chased his nemesis through a carnivalesque parade of the Day of Dead that featured huge *papier mâché* skeletons and skulls, and thousands of people dressed up and painted in similar motifs strolling and partying. The Mexican government had paid millions for the sequence to be filmed in the capital. The problem was that no such thing as a 'spectacular parade of the Day of Dead' existed. Eager to reap the rewards of the 'branding' investment, the city's Secretary of Tourism therefore suggested inventing 'a carnival of the Day of the Dead, because with the James Bond movie, tourists will want to come and see it and they will not find it' (Torres Ramos 2018: 75). And so it happened that in 2016 the first 'Desfile [parade] of the Day of Dead' was organized, for which the props of *Spectre* were reused. A new tradition was invented, and it became an instant success. The 2023 parade attracted thousands of participants and more than a million spectators who watched a folkloric parade of skulls, skeletons, impersonations of Aztec deities associated with Mictlán, and the like.

This recent cultural phenomenon shows how global cultural images are localized, how traditions are always made and remade, and how distinctive cultural images and narratives become intertwined. Unsurprisingly, these cultural imageries are also mobilized by Santa Muerte devotees and the cult's organic intellectuals.[5] The Day of the Dead (as opposed to Day of 'Death') and the iconic dressed female skeleton known as the Catrina are well-known Mexican emblems. While the subject of successful state-led constructions of Mexican culture's alleged intimacy with death as a national totem during the twentieth century, 'a densely-layered repertoire of death rituals and death vocabularies had already developed' and shaped state and popular culture alike (Lomnitz 2005: 58). In recent years, commercialization blurred the boundaries between Day of the Dead and Catrina imagery and practices.

The Día de Muertos is the Mexican rendering of the Catholic celebrations of All Saints' and All Souls' Days (November 1 and 2), when believers remember and honour their dead. The established liturgical requirements have become overshadowed by 'an ostentatious display of art, poetry, and creative energy', which involves home altars for the deceased and decorating grave sites (Brandes 2006: 6). One finds special sugar-coated bread and other foods on gravestone *ofrendas*, and altars adorned with paper cut-outs, orange *cempasúchitl* flowers, candies in the form of skulls. News outlets publish satirical faux epitaphs about known personalities, portraying them as skeletons

---

[5] In what follows I draw on Pansters (2019: 14–18).

to remind them, like the medieval dance macabre, of their transience. Taken together, 'in no other predominantly Catholic country in the world are All Saints and All Souls days celebrated with the kind of artistic exuberance and humor' as in Mexico (Brandes 2006: 61). For many it has become a key symbol of Mexican identity. The evidence shows that the Mexican Day of the Dead is 'a colonial invention, a unique product of colonial demographic and economic processes' (Brandes 2006: 40). Postconquest death, destruction, and suffering in New Spain's ethnically complex society transformed an originally sober Catholic mortuary ritual into something different. By the mid-eighteenth century the Day of the Dead had acquired its distinctive expressions in New Spain, an evolution that heightened from the second half of the nineteenth century onwards.

Around 1900, politically inspired graphic illustrations in broadsides and the penny press became popular. Part of an emergent urban print culture, these publications addressed everyday events and mocked elite corruption and hypocrisy. Close to the Day of the Dead, they printed so-called satirical ballads and witty rhymes – called *calaveras* (skulls) – illustrated with engravings of 'vivid and lively skeletons and skulls' (Wollen 1989: 14–15). They became channels for dissident political views. José Guadalupe Posada (1852–1913), the most renowned and creative engraver of the time, has become best known for the 'burlesque vitality' of his *calaveras* (Perdigón 2008: 44). His image of the Catrina stuck out as emblematic: the skull of a 'society belle' with an elegant hat adorned with feathers and flowers. Posada's dancing skeletons soon gained a lasting influence on Mexican visual culture and popular art. Appreciative of figurative folk art, his work dovetailed with Mexico's (post)revolutionary ideologies of national identity. By the 1930s, 'Posada and his *calaveras* had become symbolic for Mexico', and the skeleton achieved its totemic status (Brandes 2006: 63; Lomnitz 2005: 419). In recent decades, a more stylized Catrina has risen to prominence in the commodified world of tourism and branding things Mexican. Alongside the Day of the Dead, Posada's humanized skeletons have become part of Mexico's cultural and iconographic reservoir, forming distinct, albeit related, mortuary imageries that are often perceived as, and reduced to, 'one undifferentiated syndrome' (Brandes 2006: 66).

The latter is also relevant for the Santa Muerte cult since it is often assumed to be another expression of a purported Mexican preoccupation with death and the dead. While pre-Hispanic deities of death, the Day of the Dead, Posada's Catrinas, and Santa Muerte should not be understood as externalizations of some cultural essence, meaningful cultural conversations among them take place. Shaped by shifting social and political forces, these conversations are practices through which meanings, symbols, and images can transit from one place to another (Lamrani 2022). For example, Santa Muerte's present-day three-dimensional iconography may be the outcome of the coalescence of early two-dimensional Santísima Muerte prayer card images and the playful attributes associated with Catrina puppets (Kristensen 2016). While the emic account at the outset of this section linked Santa Muerte, pre-Hispanic deities, and the Day of the Dead, historical research shows that the origins and features of Santa Muerte devotion are indeed embedded in broad symbolic reservoirs and conversations.

Ethnographic Encounters

Questions about the origins of current Santa Muerte devotion also arose when anthropologists conducted ethnographic fieldwork at altars and recorded devotees' first-hand experiences and histories. The findings tell us something about moments, places, and forms of Santa Muerte devotion during the twentieth century. For example, the memories of a prominent shrine owner and an early anthropologist talk about devotional practices during the early 1960s and 1970s (Alba Vega & Braig 2022: 552; Perdigón 2008). Another anthropologist situated the beginnings of the cult's expansion in Veracruz in 1993, the same year mentioned for Tuxtla Gutiérrez, home to San Pascualito (Flores Martos 2007; Bolaños Gordillo 2015). Yet another chronicled the origins in Chetumal (Quintana Roo) back to at least 1986 (Higuera Bonfil 2015b). In 1992, Thompson (1998) acquired his first Santa Muerte prayer card in the border town of Nogales. A few years later he found them in the United States. In Michoacán, devotional traces go back to the 1960s (Vargas González 2004), while Olavarrieto Marenco (1977) came across booklets with prayers for 'erotic magic' in the Tuxtlas region (Veracruz) in the early 1970s. Devotees in Mexico City nowadays worship the skeletal San Bernardo found underneath a house in Tepatepec (Hidalgo) in 1965 as the oldest Santa Muerte statue (Kristensen 2016).

There are, however, earlier reports about the cult. During fieldwork in the 1950s in the northern Laguna region Isabel Kelly found 'santa muerte' prayer cards (1965: 108). Based on late 1950s fieldwork in Mexico City, Oscar Lewis's celebrated *The Children of Sánchez* contains the story of Marta and her husband Crispín, who is physically abusive and a womanizer. To put an end to his philanderings and return him 'beaten and tied, to fulfil his promises', Marta was advised to pray to Santa Muerte for nine consecutive nights (Lewis 1961: 289–91). Frances Toor's monumental *A Treasury of Mexican Folkways* (1947) also mentions Santa Muerte in relation to love magic. Ethnographic findings from the 1940s through the 1970s all highlight the role of women in Santa Muerte devotion in secluded domestic spaces.

There is also evidence of Santa Muerte worship in the confined environment of Mexican prisons. Kristensen (2015) concluded that in Mexico City this started during the 1990s, when incarcerations rose sharply. A criminological study claimed that all over the national prison system the Santísima Muerte cult was practised, including at the Islas Marías federal prison 100 kilometres off Mexico's western coast (Payá 2006: 243; Goldman 2014: 207). Already during the early 1970s one female prisoner stumbled upon a fellow inmate's Santa Muerte altar (Denegri 1978: 29). In the twenty-first century, Yllescas (2018, 2023) has amply documented Santa Muerte devotion in prisons and hypothesized that this is where the cult's origins lie.

In sum, ethnographic research carried out over several generations has rendered evidence of nascent Santa Muerte devotional practices in the secluded environments of private homes and prisons across the country during the second half of the twentieth century; so far nothing earlier than the 1940s has emerged. The nascent cult involved the circulation of prayer cards, which gradually gave way to small self-made images and altars from the 1970s onwards. Before the mid-1990s the cult had made few inroads into public space, but by 2008, the Mexico City metropolitan area alone was estimated to house around 300 street altars (Kristensen 2015: 8). It seems that after the Santa Muerte cult 'went public' central Mexico became its heartland.

Santa Muerte Origins: Many Tributaries and a Master Template

Such a complicated cultural phenomenon is bound to speak to a variety of social and religious historical backgrounds and cultural complexes that require diverse approaches, perspectives, and methodologies. Several conclusions can be drawn. First, reporting the origins of Santa Muerte devotion is by no means the privileged terrain of anthropologists, historians, or investigative journalists. Devotees and cult leaders have long and actively engaged in creating their own historical narratives and mythologies.

Moreover, investigating the origins of the Santa Muerte cult requires distinguishing between ethnographic accounts of nascent devotional practices since the 1940s, and broader, indirect historical and religious antecedents that shaped and nurtured it in diverse ways. The former suggested various explanatory directions: the Santa Muerte cult evolved from that of San Pascualito, its roots are in rural indigenous communities that fed rural-urban migration after 1950, or in the (urban) prison system. While these specific historical hypotheses don't exclude the role of broader cultural forces in the cult's genealogy, they have empirical and explanatory constraints of their own. Prisons played a key role in the development of the cult, but the earliest ethnographical evidence of Santa

Muerte devotion centred on love and family matters rather than on prisoners' concerns with justice. The rural indigenous communities-migration hypothesis is promising but its empirical base is still narrow. Moreover, it cannot explain why the current Santa Muerte cult appears to be above all an urban phenomenon. Has research had an urban bias?

The ethnographic insights into the cult's material and devotional aspects during the decades prior to its spectacular growth and visibility after 2000 also prompted research about historical and religious antecedents. Corroborating the historical links between early and late colonial phenomena and sources, and the emergence of the Santa Muerte cult since the mid-twentieth century is, however, hampered by the scarcity of reliable sources. Assessing these historiographic gaps requires the systematic review of colonial and nineteenth-century governmental and church archives. In terms of Santa Muerte devotional practices, the evidence of their pedigrees in the country's rich history of Catholic folk saints, shrines, and miraculous images is compelling. Sections 2 and 3 examine this further.

Finally, essential features of the contemporary Santa Muerte cult are also embedded in traditions of mortuary imagery, especially the Catholic but increasingly secularized Day of the Dead celebrations, and late-nineteenth-century secular imageries of the *calaveras* and the Catrina. These cultural repertoires dovetailed with postrevolutionary nationalist ideologies and policies, metamorphosed into prime symbols of national identity, and paved the way for the skeleton achieving its totemic status in Mexico. As such they shape Santa Muerte iconography and ritual, not least because ordinary devotees participate in the conversations and narratives about the cult's origins.

2 Material Culture and Spaces of Santa Muerte Devotion

Many stalls in the Juárez market in Monterrey, northern Mexico's industrial powerhouse, are crammed with a colourful assortment of commodities used in popular religious and esoteric rituals: statues, lotions, candles, soap, necklaces, booklets, and more. Outside the market I noticed two young men with a huge Santa Muerte effigy. Although entirely covered in plastic wrap, its remarkable design was easily appreciated: the saint's robe was completely plastered with (fake) dollar bills and trimmed with golden piping (Figure 3).

The men had just purchased the statue and waited for their pickup truck to take it home. While spectacular for its size, the 'dollar' Santa Muerte is not that difficult to come across. Near Mexico City's historical centre, a curious sidewalk altar contains a dollar Santa Muerte flanked by two other popular saints.

Figure 3 Statue of Santa Muerte, near Juárez market, in Monterrey. Photo by Javier A. Orellana Pérez.

If today's devotees decide to acquire a Santa Muerte figurine, they can choose from a bewildering supply of designs, sizes, colours, materials, and scenes. Well-stocked esoteric market stalls make up a trove of visual exuberance and symbolic enjoyment. This section examines the main features of Santa Muerte material culture and argues that its vibrancy and expressive diversity is propelled by grassroots devotional agency. It specifically looks at how statue designs, gender identity, and tattooing are related to the creative diversification and personalization of devotion. After that, it focuses on different places of devotion, and the services offered. Most attention goes to physical altars and shrines, but online space is also considered.

Santa Muerte Images: Diversity, Intimacy, and Family

In their classic design, commercially produced Santa Muerte statuettes come as skeletons with bold skulls dressed in hooded robes. Their size may vary from an impressive two metres to tiny two centimetres. Many figurines at home altars, which devotees often bring to public rituals, measure between twenty and fifty centimetres. Easily transported, these are generally made in one piece from plastic, alabaster, or resin, but also *papier mâché* and occasionally wood. In prisons many are made of soap.

The limbs and skulls, but above all the robes, come in symbolically charged colours: a red painted Santa Muerte is thought to be helpful in matters of the heart, a gold-coloured one for financial fortune, a green one for legal matters, amber for physical and mental health, and blue for professional well-being and wisdom. An entirely white figurine represents purification and is employed to discharge negative energies. The black Santa Muerte allegedly provides total protection, but some turn to her to inflict harm on others. Since devotees often face assorted challenges, the multicoloured Santa Muerte statue – known as the 'seven powers' – has become very popular (Figure 4). Colours are meant to steer Santa Muerte's force in desired directions.[6] Some statues are painted with

Figure 4 The multicoloured 'seven powers' Santa Muerte, Juárez market, Monterrey. Photo by author.

---

[6] General agreement exists about the meanings of the main colours, but there is no codified sample card.

more frivolous concepts in mind: on the outskirts of Ciudad Juárez I once encountered a Santa Muerte that sported Guadalajara's Chivas soccer club robe!

Colourful diversity is a relatively recent phenomenon. Before 2000 the range of representations of Santa Muerte was much more limited. Since the turn of the century, the expansion of what anthropologist Antonio Higuera Bonfil (2020) called the 'chromatic possibilities' has been intimately connected to the cult's increasing public visibility, that is, the manifestation of 'iconic aspirations' and the crystallization of a religious icon with 'the capacity to enshrine and convey a sense of a special, sacrosanct presence to beholders' (Beekers & Tamimi Arab 2016; Knott et al. 2016: 129). It offered devotees opportunities to express their specific needs. The meanings of the colour palette started to circulate in Santa Muerte DIY guides (Velázquez 2005).

Iconic differentiation is further enhanced by the objects that accompany Santa Muerte statues and symbolize her powers. The most recognizable attribute, reminiscent of the classic Grim Reaper, is the scythe – occasionally a sword – that symbolizes the saint's ability – not the decision which is God's – to cut the thread of life. But it may also represent harvesting crops and therefore prosperity and hope. Santa Muerte often carries a globe in her left hand, denoting that she holds power over all things living. Her left hand may also carry the scales of justice, which represents fairness, impartiality, and ultimately the democratic nature of death. Unsurprisingly, Santa Muerte is also known as *La Justiciera* (She who does justice). Symmetrical scales can signal the saint's ability to provide stability, harmony, and interior peace. Other objects include an hourglass, a lantern, and an owl. Standing on the saint's shoulder or near her feet is the owl, a symbolically complex animal that can be an emblem of carnal desire, but also signifies the soundless bird showing the way through darkness, a symbol of wisdom, and *venturi nuntia luctus* (a messenger of grief).[7]

Innovative designs and settings of Santa Muerte statuettes have brought additional objects into play, boosting iconographic variation. The popular saint dressed in a pre-Hispanic outfit is a good example. In addition to the scythe and the globe, the latter comes with an impressive, feathered head decoration, as well as with disks attached to the shoulders with images of pyramids and snakes. But there are others. Sprawling wings have been added to Santa Muerte images, which in some cases are said to protect sex workers (Higuera Bonfil 2020: 133). The winged Santa Muerte, also known as the 'Angel of Death', became popular after it appeared in a Harry Potter film

---

[7] Ovid, *Metamorphoses*, book V, 549–50, translation at: www.perseus.tufts.edu/hopper/text?doc=Perseus%3Atext%3A1999.02.0029%3Abook%3D5%3Acard%3D487.

(Perdigón & Robles Aguirre 2019). She may also appear on a motorcycle, or on horseback, which devotees tend to identify as apocalyptic. The unmediated equivalence between Maria, mother of Jesus, and Santa Muerte represented in a 'pietà' Santa Muerte is mesmerizing (Figure 5). Outside a shrine in San Luis Potosí, visitors encounter a massive black Santa Muerte seated in a gold-coloured throne adorned with winged dragons, a scythe in her right hand and on her lap the ivory-coloured corpse of Jesus Christ with his crown of thorns and stigmata. To its right is a large mural of a grisly looking Santa Muerte in a blue tunic as well as a large wooden crucifix. Together they form an impressive composition of Santa Muerte material culture. Commercially produced smaller pietà effigies are sold across Mexico.

A final layer of Santa Muerte's iconographic lavishness is added by dressing up prefabricated statuettes. Building upon a long Catholic tradition to dress female saints during festive occasions, Santa Muerte devotees may decorate their images with gowns, jewellry, and wigs. For example, the main figure in doña Enriqueta Romero's famous shrine in Mexico City is renowned for her collection of gowns and excessively long hair. The acquisition of dresses or wigs is a way to express devotees' gratitude for a particular saintly intervention – or to formulate

Figure 5 'Pietà' Santa Muerte, San Luis Potosí. Photo by author.

a petition – but is also common at anniversaries of shrines. 'It's a way to be grateful for all one has already received. It's a way to celebrate ... reward, thank [her]; dressing her is a gift', as one prominent devotee put it (Perdigón 2015: 48). The designs and colours of the garments are carefully selected on aesthetic and symbolic grounds. Embellishing Santa Muerte often involves adding accessories such as handbags, umbrellas, gloves, hats, and crowns (Reyes Ruiz 2010). Since people may spend considerable resources on them, a specialized cottage industry has emerged (Perdigón 2015: 60). Seamstresses are contracted for their technical skills and ritual knowledge that enhances the dressed saint's spiritual power (Mancini 2015).

Just as material artefacts not only enshrine meanings and values but also engender experiences and feelings, so does dressing up have performative and identity-making effects (Knott et al. 2016: 128). It enhances the personalization of the saintly figure and expresses the particularity of a Santa Muerte–devotee relationship. The devotee's desires bestow upon the saint a personality beyond her generic representation, creating a space of ownership and intimacy, a key feature of current Santa Muerte devotion (Yllescas 2013: 72). Like the chromatic explosion noted before, this also is a relatively recent phenomenon. Scant ethnographic material about the underground period of devotion indicates the existence of modest, private altars with two-dimensional Santa Muerte prayer cards and posters. From the 1980s and early 1990s onwards these morphed into three-dimensional effigies (Kristensen 2011: 83–4). In 1995, at the Sonora market in Mexico City, plastic Santa Muerte statues measuring from five to forty centimetres were for sale (Thompson 1998). A few years later, human-size statues were circulating. While nowadays all private and public sites of worship are organized around three-dimensional sculptures, the surrounding walls are still covered with posters and paintings. One has not replaced the other.

The transformation of two-dimensional images into three-dimensional objects had far-reaching consequences for the organization and experience of devotional practices. The shift became a vehicle for extending agency and meaning-making (Pansters 2019: 33). While two-dimensional images can only be appreciated by eyesight, statues allow touching, hugging, dancing, decorating, and dressing, which can be observed at public ceremonies when devotees bring their own statuettes. Kristensen has stressed that 'the statues, and particularly their eyes, conjure up a hidden inner world' (2016: 412). Three-dimensional figurines enable devotees much better to weld durable personal, intimate, and familial relationships.

Many devotees experience and speak of Santa Muerte as part of their family and daily life, as shown in Sergio de la Fuente's (2015) moving portrait of Carlos and Youalli, who run the Casa Esotérica de los Santos in a market in southern Mexico City. At its entrance stands a human size 'dollar' Santa Muerte. As Carlos, Youalli, and their children practically spend their entire lives in the market and at home with 'their' *Santita*, they see her as part of the family. When their seven-year-old son says goodbye to the saint, he gives her a high-five and kisses the skull (De la Fuente 2015: 71). Most devotees cherish an intimate relationship with Santa Muerte and attribute to her quintessentially human psychological properties, such as mood swings, whims, and impulses. She can be humble and compelling, caring and loving, but also demanding and vengeful. The latter is the subject of debate: some devotees emphasize the saint's tolerance and understanding, others believe that when not treated properly, she may behave like a 'high-maintenance *cabrona* [bitch]' (Roush 2014: 145). As a family member, she is loyal and will defend her kin. In addition, Santa Muerte is believed to need food, beverages, and clothing, and occasionally enjoys a cigarette and a tequila. For one informant, the likeness of humans and the saint is obvious: 'we always have death with us, we carry her inside of us, in our bones'. Corporeal similitude obliterates the saint's non-human origins. Santa Muerte appears 'as a *'humanized* God-object ... that requires to be fed and kept happy so that she keeps her promises' (Perdigón 2008: 78–9).

In sum, the critical transformation of two- into three-dimensional material representations of Santa Muerte and their unrestricted iconographic diversification at the end of the twentieth century prompted processes of personalization and humanization. While interconnected, they constitute two distinct dimensions: while personalization refers to fashioning Santa Muerte identities and devotee–saint relationships according to individual needs and *gustos*, humanization refers to the generic conceptualization of the saint as a human-like member of the family, who deserves to be treated correspondingly.

Gender: Materiality and Meanings

The personalization and humanization of Santa Muerte have overwhelmingly and unambiguously underscored the saint's female identity. Devotees point at historical precedents and match the saint with La Parca, the Spanish female equivalent of the Grim Reaper, an allegory of death that migrated from Europe to colonial Spanish America. Yet present-day devotional practices are far more important. Dressing up and beautifying the saint accentuate her femininity. Some statues are designed to bring out female bodily contours. Others are modelled after Posada's flirtatious Catrinas, exemplifying symbolic cross-fertilization. One scholar observed 'seductive' depictions of the saint exposing her tibia and femur (García Zavala 2007: 222). Perhaps the most compelling iconographic expression of female gender is a pregnant Santa Muerte. In Ciudad

Juárez, I once encountered a homemade pregnant Catrina-like statue in a long purple evening dress, while art historian Caroline Perrée spotted a prefabricated figurine displaying a transparent foetus-carrying womb (2016: 216).

Dressing up Santa Muerte statuettes in elegant clothing and accessories endorses her beauty. One devotee said: '[S]piritually, she is beautiful, because she gives me strength, peace, balance. ... And physically as well, for [her] beauty is natural as it was created by God' (Perdigón 2015: 57). Unsurprisingly, one of her most common pet names is *La Niña Bonita* (The Pretty Girl). Many other monikers using the feminine noun are in use, for example *La Blanquita* (The White Girl), *La Flaca* (The Skinny Girl), and *La Dama Poderosa* (The Powerful Lady). The gendering effects of Santa Muerte naming cannot be underestimated.

Santa Muerte's gender is furthermore articulated by describing her as a female family member: a (little) sister (*hermana, hermanita*); a child (*nena, niña*); a mother (*madre* or *madrecita*); a godmother (*madrina*); or as the informal but loving *manita* (female friend or a young female sibling). Tenderly talking about Santa Muerte underscores her prominent role in the family life of devotees. Other female identities used in Santa Muerte iconography are the princess or the queen, the *quinceañera*, or the bride, all in matching attire. The main statue of the appropriately called 'Santuario a la Niña Blanca' in Ciudad Juárez is a seated bride in a white wedding gown, bridal veil, and tiara.

Embellishing their Santa Muerte statuettes with exuberant tailor-made dresses, wigs, and other accessories to flaunt her inner and outer beauty, addressing her in gender-specific diminutives, and regarding her as a close family member, doesn't mean devotees intend to soften or nullify her ghastly countenance. More than a protective and caring Maria figure, she is above all seen as purposeful, potent, and effective, as a *Dama Poderosa* (Chesnut 2012: 8). When in 2007 the leader of the influential Iglesia Católica Tradicional México–USA shrine in Mexico City replaced the classic skeleton Santa Muerte with a dulcified and incarnated 'Angel of Death' that, according to some, too much resembled the leader's wife, devotees didn't buy it, and abandoned the congregation (Roush 2014: 137). While embedded in Catholic traditions, Santa Muerte hardly embodies the traditional Catholic gender values of the *marianismo* complex (Navarro 2002). In contrast to the stereotypical self-sacrificing woman, Santa Muerte projects a countercultural message.

The Body as Altar

A particular materialization of the saint's rich iconography, tattoos are extraordinary vehicles of the individualization of devotion. Many, perhaps even most, devotees bear tattoos. Once etched on the skin, a tattoo is a long-lasting indicator of one's beliefs. In contrast to most other material artefacts, with their tattoos devotees always carry Santa Muerte and her protection with them. This can be opportune: who would point a knife at the Santa Muerte tattooed on the back of a fellow prisoner? Moreover, visible tattoos are deployed as an unconventional medium to intervene in public space (Gamboa 2010). In addition, getting a tattoo is painful, which is a unique way to express devotional commitment.

What explains the significance of tattooing as a vehicle for individualization? First, there is the notion that tattoos turn bodies into Santa Muerte altars. Inevitably, a physically embodied material icon epitomizes a personalized connection between the devotee and the saint. In 2022, a devotee explained to me that to be meaningful a tattoo's design and bodily place should emerge from within.[8]

Second, a decision to get a Santa Muerte tattoo sets in motion personalized and symbolically charged choices. The first concerns determining its specific purpose: a petition, an expression of gratitude, or evoking a significant experience. Then a devotee selects a tattoo design. Next comes the symbolically and aesthetically meaningful decision about the tattoo's bodily location. Certain features, such as size or design, may be adjusted to certain body parts so that their shape and hypodermic structure enhance the tattoo's quality. A Santa Muerte tattoo on the side of her lower legs was meant to keep Blanca on the right path in life, while a tattoo on the front of Mónica's left arm kept the saint always at her side (Perdigón & Robles Aguirre 2019: 166). Trusting its protective effectiveness, Genaro promised his back as an altar to the saint (Yllescas 2018: 168).

Even if design categories and image typologies circulate among devotees and tattoo artists, the individual choices at each of the different steps make up for an immensely diverse universe of Santa Muerte tattoos, partly enriched by popular cultural crossovers, such as films, album covers, fashion hypes, and so on. The popularity of tattoos in today's world dovetailed with personalized Santa Muerte material culture and devotional practices. Perhaps more than other material, commercially produced artefacts, tattoos etched on unique living bodies exemplify a key feature of intimate and effervescent Santa Muerte devotion.

Private Altars

If tattoos transform bodies into altars, devotees have been equally busy erecting physical altars across Mexico and beyond during the first two decades of the twenty-first century. I will concentrate on different physical spaces of worship,

---

[8] Interview with Juan Antonio, Mexico City, 27 July 2022.

and the services offered there. In generic terms, an altar is a consecrated relational space with objects and images through which human beings establish and embody a connection with a transcendental entity.

It is important to recall that during most of the twentieth century, Santa Muerte worship was concealed. Since 2000, however, things have changed dramatically. Today, Santa Muerte devotional practices and rituals overwhelmingly take place in private *and* public spaces. The key distinction resides in the fact that the former are, in principle, only accessible for individual devotees and a few trusted others, generally a family, whereas the latter are open to everybody. Although in the real world the boundaries separating them are dynamic, to organize my findings the distinction is helpful. Even in Mexican prisons inmates distinguish between the private altars in their cells and the public ones in the common spaces and corridors (Yllescas 2018: 133–8).

Most Santa Muerte devotees have private self-made altars in their homes, and/or in their workspaces, and many also participate in ceremonies at public altars or shrines. Private altars vary enormously in terms of size, complexity, and lavishness. A table placed against a wall can be the basic structure, but people may also use narrow shelves. In 2022, I visited a couple's very small apartment without a clearly identifiable altar, but with many different-sized statues everywhere, as if the entire three-by-three-metre room made up an altar. Most private altars possess one central Santa Muerte effigy, surrounded by other images and objects, such as candles and offerings. Some are large and crowded, others are modest or stylized. Setting up a private altar occurs according to personal preferences and finances. Altars are dynamic and diverse places that expand and evolve. Since the mid-2000s, guidelines for constructing an altar have widely circulated in magazines, booklets, and the internet. For example, *El libro de la Santa Muerte* (Anonymous 2007b: 25–30) provides extensive instructions on proper fabrication, placement, and consecration of the altar. Although devotees use these guidelines, the room for personal choices and convictions is wide. For example, instructions that a private altar should be the exclusive domain of Santa Muerte is disregarded by many devotees. Despite the spectacular visibility of public shrines, the significance of private altars for Santa Muerte devotees should be highlighted. A leading specialist on rituals and theology once stressed the bottom-up and anti-institutional orientation of the cult when he wrote that 'your [private] altar destined to Her' is the most valuable place of worshipping (Valadez 2005a: 7). Just as in the case of material objects, private altars are key spaces for fashioning intimate personalized devotion.

Public Altars and Shrines

Most scholars agree that when it comes to public or street altars there is a 'before and after' Enriqueta Romero's decision in September 2001 to place a large Santa Muerte statue outside her house. The story has become a key chapter in the history and mythology of the cult. After one of her sons was unexpectedly released from prison he gave her a human-sized statue of the saint. After all, she had pressed him to ask Santa Muerte for protection in prison and for a positive outcome of his court case. When the statue arrived at the family's home in Alfarería Street in Mexico City, it became difficult to accommodate (Kristensen 2016: 402–3). Doña Queta, as she is widely known, recalled that she eventually asked her husband to construct an outside altar for the sizeable effigy (Alba Vega & Braig 2022: 553). Passersby and visitors started to leave offerings and candles and soon the Romero family altar had become a street altar.

Today, doña Queta's altar is Mexico's most famous, photographed, and filmed Santa Muerte altar, not least because she initiated monthly rosaries here (see Section 3). While this was not necessarily the first street altar, the turning point for the emergence of public Santa Muerte devotion is what occurred in Alfarería Street in September 2001. Between 2001 and 2008 the number of public altars in the greater metropolitan area mushroomed from fewer than 10 to around 300 (Kristensen 2015). Similar developments occurred elsewhere; the city of San Luis Potosí had at least five public shrines in 2008, and one held monthly rosaries (Leija Parra 2010: 80–2).

Public altars are open for all devotees; some can be visited for worshipping twenty-four hours a day, all week long; others have opening hours. Two basic types can be distinguished. The first one is an elementary, usually open-air structure at a street corner, the extension of a house, or a market stall. A good example is the small but elaborate street corner altar I visited in the southern part of Mexico City. It consists of a 1.5-metre-wide glass case that sits on a brick base. The case is crammed with Santa Muerte statues, and assorted offerings around the central skeleton effigy. Before the case stands a small prie-dieu. The altar is equipped with camera surveillance. In 2006, in a San Luis Potosí market, a modest altar accidentally came into being as devotees left candles, flowers, and petitions at a large statue the market stall owners had planned to sell (Leija Parra 2010: 67).

A more spectacular case of appropriating public space and claiming visibility is the altar constructed by the Congregación Nacional de la Santa Muerte in Ecatepec. Congregation leaders first placed a Santa Muerte statue on a pedestal underneath a large overpass. Devotees then fenced off the new place of worship with stones – providing 'a circle of divine protection'. The altar subsequently occupied the entire space below the overpass with additional pedestals and statues. In 2018, painting the overpass pillars black incorporated them into the altar structure, while a tall gold-coloured iron fence entirely enclosed what had evolved into a demarcated and recognized sacred urban space (Valverde Montaño 2020: 138–42).

The second type of public altar is a roofed construction built for that purpose. Visitors must enter to see the actual effigies. They allow more privacy to devotees. Constructions vary enormously in size and design. Although some scholars have proposed more refined categorizations, devotees themselves tend to use the Spanish terms *altar*, *templo*, *santuario*, or *capilla* rather randomly (Higuera Bonfil 2018: 406). Emic nomenclature hardly provides systematic distinctions in the diversity of public street altars or closed shrines. A *templo* in Guadalajara used to be a warehouse (Bravo Lara 2013: 22). The Santa Muerte 'Martita' *santuario* in Ciudad Juárez consists of two separate buildings in a large yard. At the desert highway junction of El Huizache, the 'Capilla de la Santa' could not differ more from the nearby 'Capilla de la Santa Muerte'.

The distinction between private, that is, domestic, and public altars – in their two basic formats – has an analytical value but should not be objectified. In real-life devotional practices, the boundaries are experienced as porous and dynamic in several ways. Intermediate spaces between private and public spheres exist when members of a particular community (not being family) interact with the saint. A good example is a workspace. In the historical mining town of Sombrerete, miners placed a wooden Santa Muerte figurine at the entrance of the pit, to whom they commend their souls before descending to work (Anonymous 2007a: 9). In addition, devotional practices continuously establish and renew linkages between both spaces. Many devotees regularly bring their domestic statues to public gatherings. The magazine *Devoción a la Santa Muerte* interviewed a young man with an impressive private altar, but who also 'took his girls [*sus niñas*] out on the streets' during the whole month, attending ceremonies at different public shrines (Anonymous 2005b: 18). Supplies for private altars are acquired at esoteric shops or public shrines. In other words, common devotional practices constitute an interactional space between private and public altars.

Social relations among members of local Santa Muerte communities also contribute to blurring boundaries. A woman who for many years successfully ran an esoteric market stall extended invitations to clients to visit her private 'apartment-altar-sanctuary' (De la Fuente 2016: 169). In another case, a couple and their young children lived in a modest apartment with their family altar. At one point, some friends and relatives asked permission to visit the altar and solicit Santa Muerte's help. This put the young family on a path towards offering a public space for worshipping, without losing its private altar functions (Higuera Bonfil 2018). Finally, the dynamics of the private-public identity of altars is at least partly driven by the political forces that push for the cult's institutionalization. This is because becoming part of larger Santa Muerte networks or organizations bolsters private-public hybridization (see Section 4).

A distinctive feature of public altars is that they are not only places for individual or collective worship but also for selling a wide range of commodities and spiritual services. These include cleansings (*limpias*) of people, homes, or offices, as well as marriage counselling. In southern Mexico and Guatemala – which have overwhelmingly indigenous populations – cult leaders are perhaps first *curanderos* (healers), who draw on a wide range of religious and spiritual traditions (García Astorga 2016; Michalik 2011). The services offered at an altar in Chetumal on the Caribbean coast included the preparation of potions and black magic (Higuera Bonfil 2015a). In a shrine along the northern Mexico–US border, different spiritual services, including so-called *amarres* (love-binding spells), were on offer for 150 pesos (US$8 at the time).[9] Meanwhile, Ismael, a young man in charge of the rosaries at a shrine in Mexico City, spiritually assists believers with Tarot readings. Over the years he also specialized in *amarres de amor*. Ismael also does 'energetic cleansings' to purify clients from the negative elements accumulated in their stressful life in the metropolis.[10]

Santa Muerte in Digital Space

Although Santa Muerte devotees resort to Ismael's street corner altar for diverse services, over the years he has obtained an online, transnational clientele and developed ways to carry out *limpias* through his Facebook page. Not least because of its visual qualities, the online presence of Santa Muerte devotion is widespread and manifold. The internet allows many formats with information about the cult – websites, blogs, podcasts, YouTube, TikTok, and social media. A Google search renders millions of hits, many linked to commercial sites. Others are used by devotees or cult leaders to disseminate information about the history of the cult, and its iconographic and theological features and rituals. This information once circulated in booklets and magazines. There is a lot of copying and pasting. When a Santa Muerte novice wants information about how to set up a domestic altar, the internet is the place they go. In this sense, online information plays a significant role in diffusing or marketing the cult. At the end of a visit to a Guadalajara shrine, the owner asked a colleague and me about our thoughts about his shrine, filmed our reactions with his phone, and immediately

---

[9] Fieldnotes, Santuario Santísima Muerte 'Martita', Ciudad Juárez, 31 July 2016.
[10] Interview with Ismael, Mexico City, 9 March 2023.

posted it on his Facebook account. He showed us other posts about interested people and journalists, who had visited his *templo*.[11] To counteract negative mainstream framings of the cult, the spiritual leader of the Congregación Nacional de la Santa Muerte from Ecatepec has long been active in posting content on his own YouTube channel.[12]

As Ismael's online service delivery shows, the internet provides a platform for communication between cult leaders and devotees. This proved particularly significant during the COVID-19 pandemic, when several congregational leaders communicated with their members online and transmitted live devotional rituals. For congregations with different chapters in Mexico and abroad, such as Santa Muerte Internacional, this helped to enhance the sense of belonging to a larger congregational community and to support devotees in difficult times. Although certainly not new, the pandemic boosted the cult's online presence, much of which has continued in some form after the pandemic.

For years, social media has provided excellent opportunities for online interactions and conversations. Excluding commercial sites, in 2014, Pérez Salazar & Gervasi (2015: 148) found sixty-five Santa Muerte Facebook pages, the majority of which showed low levels of interactions. Since then the number has increased. Devotees use their social media accounts to pose questions about Santa Muerte matters and obtain reactions from the group's webmaster or other devotees, often giving rise to long conversations (Torres Ramos 2017). Other devotees post words of gratitude for the saint's support, eliciting congratulatory reactions and expressions of faith. These conversations demonstrate the faith and community-building role of online religious devotion. Having said that, the same effect is also achieved in reaction to hostile interventions by non-believers in Facebook groups. These interventions indicate not only the continued existence of intolerance towards the cult but also the strengthening of Santa Muerte group identity (Pérez Salazar & Gervasi 2014, 2015).

If the manifold online presence of Santa Muerte devotion serves concrete informational, communicational, and conversational purposes, it is above all explained by their structural similarities. As I have emphasized, the dynamics of Santa Muerte devotion thrive on grassroots and decentralized agency that generates spaces for personalized and unmediated beliefs and religion-making. And because horizontal, decentralized governance, multidirectional conversations, and individual input also make up the communicative structure of the internet, especially social media, the Santa Muerte cult and the online world make perfect bedfellows (Pérez Salazar & Gervasi 2014).

---

[11] Interview with Martín, Tlaquepaque, 1 August 2022.
[12] Interview with Yamarash, Ecatepec, 12 August 2023.

3 Ritual and Theology of Santa Muerte Devotion

In Santa Muerte devotion, public shrines are places where people meet, acquire goods and services, and participate in rituals, such as rosaries and festivities. This section studies their specificities and similarities with Roman Catholic liturgies. I will show that despite the differences between shrines, a broadly shared liturgical format has developed across Mexico. At the heart of Santa Muerte beliefs and theology lies an exchange mechanism between devotees and the saint that stems from the 'management of hardships and compensatory satisfaction of worldly needs' (Graziano 2016: 16). The principal areas of petitionary concern are health, work, romance, security, and justice. But I start with a brief look at experiences that typically led devotees to visit shrines in the first place: apparitions.

Apparitions

Faced with challenging conditions, most devotees first became acquainted with Santa Muerte through family or friends. Others confronted an acute crisis, such as a serious accident or a death in the family. In hindsight, even the staunchest devotees initially hesitated to accept the recommendation to consult Santa Muerte, in view of the cult's widespread social stigma. Testimonies show that rapprochement may last years until a meaningful event sets off full devotional commitment. Practically all devotees I have spoken to over the years, including those who had been familiar with Santa Muerte since childhood, chronicle the moment and context that spurred earnest devotion. One type of such an event is an apparition.

There are many ways Santa Muerte comes to her devotees. When she appeared to Ismael in a dream, he considered himself a novice devotee. Recommended by his girlfriend's aunt he had tentatively consulted Santa Muerte to overcome a serious health issue, which he believed resulted from a curse. The episode was a breakthrough. Ismael recounts how Santa Muerte 'took over' his life – for example, her prompting him to acquire Tarot cards. At age twenty-nine he has become the key religious leader at a street altar. With his tattoos, a Santa Muerte ring, active involvement in street ceremonies, and off- and online service provision, Ismael's devotional style is outward-looking and expressive.[13]

At age 25, Alberto's life was in tatters – his marriage had collapsed, his lucrative football career had ended with a serious knee injury, and he suffered intense physical pain. He attempted suicide twice. One night he saw a woman in white slowly descending into the basement, without catching sight of her face.

---

[13] Interview with Ismael, Mexico City, 9 March 2023.

A while later the female figure, now dressed in black, returned, standing silently halfway up the stairs. Instead of fear, Alberto sensed peacefulness. However, it was not until two years later that he became a steadfast devotee, when he determined that the saint had worked hard to keep death away from him. This experience led Alberto to erect a home altar. Ever since, and in contrast to Ismael's outward-looking devotional style, he has cultivated an exceptionally private and intimate form of devotion. He has no tattoos, doesn't visit public altars, nor does he participate in rosaries. Twenty-five years later, the soft-spoken and amiable Alberto is a successful businessman.[14]

Although apparitions and encounters in dreams are not unusual, other devotees have reported that they have not 'seen' Santa Muerte but 'felt' her presence. Even though Alberto and Ismael represent different points on the spectrum of Santa Muerte devotional styles, their experiences have key elements in common. First, they had important sensorial and bodily components, something that appears to be rather common. Second, initial interactions between Santa Muerte and nascent devotees constitute intimate foundational experiences that shape people's beliefs and devotional expressions. While one erects an 'inner shrine', another embarks on a career as a local Santa Muerte guide, and a third one ends up building a large public altar. Finally, through apparitions or other bodily sensations, devotees often came to believe that it is not about devotees cozying up to Santa Muerte, but rather that Santa Muerte herself hails them as religious subjects: 'She pulls you towards her and you start to believe in her' (De la Fuente 2015: 76). It forms the basis for a rich palette of stories about 'special' devotee–saint relationships. Crediting Santa Muerte with the privilege to select potential devotees also bears out her spiritual might. Lacking institutional gatekeepers, the cult allows ample room for the reproduction of diversity and individuality.

Private Rituals

The most elementary devotional practice consists of quotidian routines. Carlos, for example, salutes his Santa Muerte every morning as an *amiga* when he opens his esoteric market stall, and his wife Youalli daily says her self-made prayer (De la Fuente 2015: 71). Renewing offerings such as candles, apples, or drinks at domestic altars every week can also be carried out in a lightly ritual fashion, understood 'as symbolic behavior that is socially standardized and repetitive' (Kertzer 1988: 9). More widely recognized as proper rituals are practices about which assorted Santa Muerte organic intellectuals have elaborated detailed scripts, and which feature a degree of formality, replicability, and

---

[14] Interview with Alberto, Tlaquepaque, 2 August 2022.

sequencing. Carrying out these rituals involves material objects, prayers, and performances to dramatically enact messages and change. These pragmatic and performative qualities are key to understanding Santa Muerte rituals as 'operational devices' that enable agency to intervene in and transform the lived environment of the devotees and the world at large (Mancini 2012).

Within the broad assortment of primarily domestic rituals carried out by a single devotee interacting with a Santa Muerte image or object, a basic distinction can be made between rituals that use certain material objects (such as incense, herbs, mirrors, or balms), and those with particular objectives (such as cleansing or warding off harmful people). An interesting example of the first type is a ritual involving herbs to help a loved one get rid of alcoholism. The devotee prepares a herbal concoction upon which the picture of the addicted person is placed with laurel leaves that are arranged in the form of a cross. The devotee then prints the name of the alcoholic, lights candles, says prayers, and requests Santa Muerte to support the addicted person in leaving the vice behind. They then bury the casserole while pronouncing: 'Santa Muerte, just as I bury this spiritual piece in your name, I invoke you to bury all my loved one's cravings and needs of the addiction' (Valadez 2005b: 11).

The use of medicinal herbs in rituals resembles shamanistic healings and cleansings. The magazine *Devoción a la Santa Muerte* regularly acknowledged the expertise of Mexico's indigenous *curanderos*, shamans, and 'spiritual brothers'. Recent ethnographic research has identified the connections between Santa Muerte devotion and indigenous healing practices, especially in southern Mexico and Guatemala (García Astorga 2016; Gutiérrez Portillo 2015; Michalik 2011). In urban Mexico, mestizo guides also engage in neo-shamanistic rituals involving Santa Muerte and the energetic force (called *nahual*) of shamans who have moved to the other world. As the entity guarding the threshold (between life and death), Santa Muerte's permission is required to transfer the energy from 'the other side' to 'charge' Santa Muerte images (Garcés Marrero 2021).

Fiestas and Rosaries: Santa Muerte's Appropriation of a Catholic Mold

Devotees tend to use emic nomenclature such as *rosarios*, *fiestas*, *ceremonias*, or *misas* when speaking about their rituals and ceremonies. While they share key features with domestic rituals, they also serve other purposes. Many, but certainly not all, devotees engage in group gatherings in addition to individual visits to street altars. For analytical purposes, I distinguish between processions, rosaries, ceremonies, and/or fiestas to celebrate the anniversary of shrines or effigies. These gatherings match traditional Roman Catholic ceremonies.

In practice, modalities often overlap, such as in the case of the large annual Santa Muerte fiesta on the 1 November 2014 – coinciding with All Saints and All Souls – in San Cristóbal de la Casas, Chiapas, recorded by Gutiérrez Portillo (2015). The event began around eight in the evening in a party centre and attracted around 600 devotees. A large provisional altar held abundant Santa Muerte effigies and offerings, such as flowers, candles, apples, prepared food, and alcoholic beverages. A vocalist read out a series of prayers. In front of the altar, the leader of the congregation, who had arrived with a black Santa Muerte statue, invited all for the ritual purification of the devotees and their effigies. Meanwhile waiters served *tamales*. After dinner, the main event of the evening took place: the coronation of Santa Muerte, which involved draping a green cloak around her, placing a crown and a scepter upon her, and sprinkling the offerings with lotion. The crowd cheered loudly, after which a dance was held to the tunes of a tropical band in honor of 'our queen, Santísima Muerte'. At other festive ceremonies, devotees not only dance in front of Santa Muerte but also take turns dancing with a Santa Muerte effigy, performing their intimate relationship with the saint (Garcés Marrero 2021: 191; Higuera Bonfil 2015b: 173). In the southeastern city of Chetumal, yearly fiestas included tropical dances, lavish alcohol consumption, and erotic performances by mostly gay male devotees to please Santa Muerte (Higuera Bonfil 2015a).

Although its combination of rosary prayers, offerings, religious rituals, dining, live music, singing, and dancing suggests that these are hybrid gatherings, organizers and devotees see them above all as fiestas, which differ from rosaries (devotional practices) properly speaking. The latter have a shorter duration, but are held regularly, mostly once a month. Rosaries at the most popular and well-known shrines may attract hundreds or even more than 1,500 devotees, whereas a small domestic–public altar may bring together a few dozen (Figure 6).

However, few will dispute that since the first street rosaries were held at the beginning of the 2000s, they have developed into the central ritual of the cult in terms of devotional and theological content and because they form a platform for group-building and identity-making. The format and content of rosaries vary between congregations and through time, but within a limited bandwidth. For example, a key component of the rosary – the Mysteries – at different shrines and moments in time is largely identical (De la Fuente 2016; Leija 2010).[15]

---

[15] The website of the *Templo de la Santa Muerte*, based in the Atlanta area, contains information about the rosary, which is identical to the ones found elsewhere. See https://c6720111209005055-8175248.yourwebsitespace.com/index, consulted 24 July 2023. The monthly *misas* of the Congregación

Figure 6 Devotees lining up and leaving Santa Muerte shrine before start of monthly rosary at Alfarería street, Mexico City. Photo by author.

Two factors explain this. Since the first open-air rosary took place at doña Queta's shrine in Tepito, its gradually emerging format and content shaped the rosaries adopted elsewhere in Mexico City and beyond. When the cult expanded publicly, no unified liturgical formats or content existed, and devotional rituals were constructed from below. Once the outline of the rosary evolved at one of the cult's most influential shrines it was replicated, with amendments, elsewhere. Second, from the beginning a key feature of the Santa Muerte rosary was its strong Catholic imprint, ranging from the concept of the rosary itself to the use of prayers as the Ave Maria, Paternoster, and Glory Be, a litany as the Agnus Dei, the use of the Mysteries, and the confession of faith (Credo). The Santa Muerte rosaries in Tepito were intelligible to Roman Catholics, which facilitated their adoption across the country (Flores Martos 2007; Kristensen 2019; Roush 2014; Valverde 2020).

In general, a Santa Muerte rosary consists of two sections: the first closely resembles original Catholic rosaries, while the second possesses a more secular though symbolically charged nature. The ceremony starts with an opening

---

Nacional de la Santa Muerte in Ecatepec have more *sui generis* features, which include the recitation of Vedic mantras, and the devotees' collective cleansing (Valverde 2020: 145–6).

prayer asking God permission to address La Santa Muerte directly (*Dios es primero*), followed by the Mysteries. In a traditional Catholic rosary, the so-called joyful, luminous, sorrowful, and glorious Mysteries recount key episodes in the life of Jesus to convey and experience the divine in earthly beings. Between 2003 and 2006, early accounts of Santa Muerte rosaries held at the Tepito shrine maintained these Catholic categories: Perdigón (2008) mentioned the five glorious Mysteries (about resurrection, ascension, etc.), whereas American anthropologist Laura Roush (2014) noted the five sorrowful Mysteries (about the agony and the scourging of Jesus, etc.), all followed by a Paternoster, ten Hail Mary's and a Glory Be. The Santa Muerte twist lay in linking the Mysteries to ordinary people's sufferings and in adding petitions from the congregation's social environment. Real-world problems of insecurity, violence, and poverty became part of the rosary. A salient example is the supplication on behalf of prisoners added to the sorrowful Mystery of Jesus's agony in the garden:

> Santísima Muerte,
> I know your power and force.
> Find an honest lawyer,
> And put him on his path.
> Santísima Muerte,
> Give him a judge,
> And show him your scales,
> So that when he adjudicates,
> He is righteous.[16]

Over time, however, in certain shrines this section of the rosary no longer referred to episodes in the life of Jesus but to episodes that bestow a divine mission upon Santa Muerte. The first Mystery tells how Our Lord the Father majestically hands to Santísima Muerte's right hand the justice-making scythe (*justiciera*). In the second Mystery, the saint receives in her right hand the entire world to protect with her benign mantle. The third Mystery states that the saint's scales are for balance and peacefulness in people's lives. The fourth Mystery tells about how the feet of Santísima Muerte descend on the earthly world to support her followers and to protect them from bad spirits and from those seeking to harm them. Finally, the fifth Mystery speaks about the window between life and death through which Santa Muerte moves back and forth when God Our Lord sends her to fetch a soul. These five Mysteries, in which God and Santa Muerte are the central protagonists, recount key episodes that elucidate the saint's might and divine roots and constitute the foundational myth or theology of the Santa Muerte cult. Each Mystery is followed by a Paternoster,

---

[16] Fragment from prayer guide, obtained from Enriqueta Romero, 1 January 2015.

a Hail Mary, a brief litany (12 times), and a joint prayer: 'That the precious and Santa Muerte, who arises from your kingdom, the temple of divine wisdom, tabernacle of divine knowledge and light of the earth, may cover us now and always. Amen' (De la Fuente 2016: 184).

The appropriation of an established Catholic format isn't limited to the mysteries. The litany of the Virgin Mary is modified by inserting references to Santa Muerte's many different titles (e.g. *Divina Santa Muerte Sanadora, Santísima Muerte Divina Caridad*, etc.) (Leija 2010: 97). The confession of guilt replaced the intercession of the Virgin Mary with that of Santa Muerte (Perdigón 2008). Heterodox creativity can also be found in Facebook communities: a 'Paternoster' to Santa Muerte becomes 'Madre Nuestra', and a 'Credo to Santísima Muerte'. The beginning of the latter reads:

> I believe in you Santísima Muerte, Justice-Making Lady,
> Mighty and Omnipotent,
> Loyal Servant of God the Father, in your hands we must
> Travel to the reunion with our Lord God ...
> I believe in you ... Santísima Muerte, who with your Scythe
> Removes every obstacle from my path, severs all evil in me,
> Who with your Divine scales settles justice in my favor,
> And with your powerful gaze protects me from all danger.
>
> (Garcés Marrero 2021: 132–4)

These examples demonstrate how ordinary devotees rewrite familiar prayers undisturbed by theological arguments but grounded in popular faith. This rosary section concludes with supplications to the saint. In small gatherings devotees may be invited to share them with others, but in larger rosaries this is done collectively either by a pastor calling for support and protection for a generic 'us' or by an invitation to all to concentrate in silence on their individual supplications.

The second section of the rosary consists of Santa Muerte's unique rites: the so-called *cadena de la fuerza* (chain of force) and the blessing of images. In the former, devotees literally connect among themselves and to the saint:

> Each person present is encouraged to take the hand of the next, to form a chain through which energy can flow. Enriqueta ... is the first in this chain, touching the altar itself. Eyes closed, we are asked to imagine Santa Muerte as a white light, to feel her coldness and how very, very close she is, to look directly at her, without fear, in our inner space, with the eyes of our soul. The leader invites the congregation to concentrate on what they want to say to her; to imagine her as intensely as possible. (Roush 2014: 136)

A long and total silence follows. At another shrine, devotees close their eyes and raise their arms towards the main Santa Muerte effigy, while the minister encourages them to concentrate on their hardships and negative feelings so that they be cleansed (Valverde 2020: 146). At yet another one, devotees raise their hands towards an effigy called *Esperanza* (Hope), praying 'give me your eyes so that I can see, your hands so that I can create', and so forth, forming 'an impressive ritual of the complete corporal identification' of the devotees with Santa Muerte (Garcés Marrero 2019: 110).

If the chain of force has a strong spiritual and social dimension, the blessing of the statuettes devotees brought along underscores the former. Again, there are interesting differences. In 2008, a rosary in San Luis Potosí attended by a few dozen devotees ended with the consecration of the statues, which consisted in blessing and cleansing them with tequila, flowers, water, and special Santa Muerte spray. In contrast, with more than a thousand people at the Tepito shrine, the blessing of the images constitutes the visual culmination of the ceremony, when all devotees lift their statues above their heads in the direction of the main shrine. As this occurs at the beginning of the evening, 'the images are illuminated and colorful, and the crowd appears not to be a mass of living persons but a crowd of grinning skeletons. In this form, the congregation becomes dazzlingly visible to itself' (Roush 2014: 136).

After one to two hours, rosary ceremonies close with final prayers and invocations, after which devotees share small presents, especially sweets, apples, prayer cards, sprays, and candles. These transactions express gratitude towards the saint, but also foster bonding and inclusion. Sometimes the shrine leaders distribute sandwiches or *tamales*, leaving behind the rosary's formal structure and giving way to joyful hustle and bustle (Perdigón 2008: 107). While many Santa Muerte devotees across Mexico and beyond regularly gather at street or indoor altars for collective ceremonies such as rosaries, some congregations also hold rituals such as weddings and baptisms. Some do regularly, others occasionally, and yet others reject them altogether. In all, however, people pray together, and muster and admire each other's Santa Muerte paraphernalia.

Community Building and Voice

Santa Muerte apparitions and homemade rituals craft intimate and personalized narratives and expressions of devotion. Public ceremonies also allow devotees to experience private moments, and to express their devotional individuality through their outfits, adornments, tattoos, and their Santa Muerte effigies. However, through collective agency, public gatherings and rituals also intervene in the world in other ways (Mancini 2012). A first effect concerns the formation and experience of a 'congregation' itself, that is, a community of devotees identified with a particular shrine and leader with distinctive devotional practices and norms.[17] Against the background of earlier private and secluded devotion, community building acquires specific significance. As people with dissimilar life histories and from diverse neighbourhoods gather around Santa Muerte and exchange beliefs, desires, and food, public rituals are not only instances of devotion but also of festive collective self-recognition and bonding.

Second, the construction of Santa Muerte communities in public space contains a political dimension. Bringing out statues, blessing them, sporting tattoos, and praying in the streets, all have the hallmarks of the politics of visibility. An altar in the street appropriates the city and says 'here I am, and I want you to know it' (Garcés Marrero 2019: 118). Against the background of stigmatizing media accounts and public disapproval, public ceremonies and rituals convey claims of recognition. Another manifestation of Santa Muerte politics of visibility are the processions organized by some congregations, in which they push carts with large statues and carry personal effigies through the streets. For example, since 2005 a major shrine in the centre of Puebla – long a bulwark of conservative Catholicism – organized anniversary processions, which have grown year after year. The congregation members walk through the colonial city centre passing by the symbolic seats of the Catholic Church and the state, while hundreds shout well-known slogans, such as '*Se ve, se siente, la Santa está presente*' (See it, feel it, the Saint is here).[18] In terms of visibility and audibility, another slogan – '*No que no, si que sí, ya volvimos a salir*' (Zero doubts, yes indeed, we're out on the street again) – articulates a contentious yet self-confident popular religious movement. These manifestations have not been without effect. Initially the municipal government refused to grant a permit for the procession, but the congregation took to the streets anyway. Over time, the municipality became more cooperative, popular skepticism diminished, and the Santa Muerte congregation increased.[19]

In sum, the public presence and pride expressed in the exuberance of fiestas, rosaries, and processions contest ignorance and prejudice, and produce community, identity, and voice. Public events are platforms for the presentation of self, political agency, and the desire to be part of a public conversation. A few

---

[17] Some congregations strictly prohibit alcohol consumption and puffing joints during ceremonies, while others have no such regulations at all.

[18] A procession in Mexico City similarly halted at the metropolitan cathedral and the national palace shouting slogans about religious and political rights (Garcés Marrero 2021: 193–7).

[19] DVDs from the 2018 and 2020 processions of the 1er. Santuario a Dios y La Santa Muerte; interview with Alfonso, Puebla, 4 August 2023.

years ago, Enriqueta Romero gave me a fascinating prayer used at rosaries written in the voice of Santa Muerte. Entitled 'For all my loyal followers', it encapsulates the cult's confidence, voice, and powers:

> I am not a diabolical being,
> Nor a satanic being.
> Much less will I take a loved one,
> If you don't live up to your promise.
> And I understand that for a good reason
> You couldn't comply on this occasion.
> However, I can help and protect you.
> Because I am an angel our Father created,
> To help serve and protect.
> I am the girl that looks at you.
> My arms that carry you.
> My hands that comfort you.
> My mantle that covers and safeguards you.
> My shadow that watches over you.
> My feet that guide you.
> My scythe that defends you.
> My world in which you live.
> My breath the air you take in.
> My scales that judge righteously.
> All this I have for you.
> Just call upon me and entrust yourself to me.
> But ask me with your heart.
> Ask me humbly.
> And I will be with you.

Devotion, Theology, and Ritual

The Santa Muerte community has not produced a theological canon or an authoritative body of programmatic texts. There are influential shrine leaders and key figures who have outlined concepts and narratives about the saint and about the content and format of devotional practices, but so far no one has succeeded, or even attempted, to compose a theological and devotional corpus. Far from logocentric, Santa Muerte popular religiosity is above all about 'doing religion'. There are no entry requirements. For the evolution of the cult, the input from ordinary devotees and local congregational leaders has been critical. In fact, a key feature has been its autonomist and frankly anti-institutional outlook and organizational structure. Manuel Valadez, a prominent contributor to the *Devoción a la Santa Muerte* magazine, once wrote that 'there is no official church to worship her, the best church is your own altar' (2005a: 7). In addition, most congregations and their leaders value their independence. An autonomist ideology and devotional practice work against the centralized instituting of theological and devotional orthodoxy. In this sense, Santa Muerte shares many features with other Latin American Catholic folk saints. The consolidation of the cult might generate pleas for firmer theological codification, but this seems unlikely now.

The critical importance of practices from below rather than scriptures from above, however, doesn't mean that Santa Muerte religiosity at large lacks coherence. The first shared theological principle is that *Dios es primero* (God comes first). Across the cult, at the start of rosaries and the like, ministers request permission from God to pray to Santa Muerte. 'She is God's servant', devotee Hortensia told Garcés Marrero (2019: 116). In the modified Mysteries, God grants Santa Muerte her symbols and might. Some congregational leaders stress that only God, not Santa Muerte, can do miracles. Most devotees will think about God as a Christian God. At Alfonso's shrine in Puebla a strong and clearly hierarchical relationship between God, the Catholic Church, and Santa Muerte constitutes its theological core, expressed in the name of the shrine, and in the key refrain that ends all prayers and adorns the altar: 'That God may bless you and that Santa Muerte may protect you, Amen' (Figure 7). The altar also displays a prominent crucifix as well as a replica of the Catholic saint El Señor de las Maravillas.

In contrast, the Congregación Nacional Santa Muerte in Ecatepec, while endorsing the 'primero Dios' principle, cultivates a universal theological discourse of God as a generic supreme power that includes non-Christian religious systems.[20] The broadly shared principle of God's supremacy also functions as a vantage point from which differences can be overcome. One Santa Muerte adherent once confided to me that while his wife had converted to Protestant Christianity, they never quarreled about religion since they agreed that 'Dios es primero'.

The second shared principle is that although she is subordinate to God, among angels, other transcendental entities, and saints, Santa Muerte is nevertheless believed to occupy a top-level position, one of God's closest and most powerful allies (Perdigón 2008: 60). This gives Santa Muerte, even if acting upon God's will, tremendous force over people. The fact that death is democratic validates this: powerful and wealthy people will also succumb to Santa Muerte's purpose. In highly unequal societies such as Mexico, the evenhandedness of death acquires distinctive meanings and imputes Santa Muerte near sovereign power. Being so close to God, Santa Muerte can intercede on behalf of her devotees.

---

[20] Interview with Yamarash, Ecatepec, 12 August 2023.

Figure 7 Main Santa Muerte statue at 1er. Santuario a Dios y La Santa Muerte, Puebla. Photo by author.

A third feature of Santa Muerte theology is that in contrast to other non-canonical saints, Santa Muerte is not identified with a particular dead person. Devotees distinguish between the generic *muerte* (death) and human *muertos* (the dead) and acknowledge that Santa Muerte never lived an earthly life. This means that she is the personification or sanctification of (the idea of) death itself. Santa Muerte is conceived as a 'spirit' who nonetheless does 'saint-like things' (Kristensen 2016: 411). While the latter justifies naming her a saint, the former explains her force and privileged position in the spiritual universe (Perdigón 2008: 60). A shrine owner in Guadalajara reframed this theological ambiguity by discriminating between Santa Muerte representing death itself and the Angel of Death, who, just like other saints, mediates between God and devotees. He worships the latter in the appropriately called Templo del Angel de la Muerte.

A fourth theological element focuses on Santa Muerte's ability to move between and connect different worlds – the sacred and the profane, the cosmos and the worldly, the living and the dead, our world and Mictlantecuhtli's netherworld. Santa Muerte appears as a liminal or mediating entity, or one that guards the threshold between distinctive but interconnected worlds. For different leaders and congregations, Santa Muerte is key for accessing divine forces or energies and, as one put it, for opening benign spiritual pathways (De la Fuente 2016). Santa Muerte guards the threshold between the *tonal* (what we are in our world) and the *nahual* (a spiritual force left by previous shamans, a dimension that cannot be known). Because *nahual* energy is considered dangerous, invoking it requires permission and protection from Santa Muerte. Once released, the *nahual* energy 'from the other side' charges Santa Muerte effigies, empowering devotee-owners to intervene in our world (Garcés Marrero 2021: 222–31).

Finally, at the core of the Santa Muerte cult at large as well as of the devotion of most other Catholic folk saints lies an exchange mechanism, and its underlying values of reciprocity, which postulates that 'devotion is structured by a spiritual contract that establishes mutual obligations for the folk saints and the devotee' (Graziano 2007: 60). Petitions to the saint come with a *manda* (promise). Failing to keep such promises after successful saintly brokerage before God may have dire consequences. What differs among saints is the subject and terms of the exchanges. Some are called upon for specific purposes, while others offer solutions to many problems. Graziano argues that devotion is 'primarily petitionary, which is to say motivated more by management of hardships and compensatory satisfaction in the here and now of worldly needs than by salvation of the soul after death' (2016: 16). Lomnitz concluded that Santa Muerte 'is not a figure of redemption, but of intervention ... Salvation in the Santa Muerte cult is no longer transcendental. It is temporary, transitory, and precarious' (2019: 190–1). In terms of format, Santa Muerte devotion closely resembles worshipping other popular Catholic saints and virgins in Mexico, including the powerful Virgin of Guadalupe.

Central to all Santa Muerte devotional practices lie the emic notions of *amparo* and *desamparo* – protection and loss or lack of protection. Also commonly used is the notion of *paro*, which indicates the interruption of some activity, but which in conjunction with 'make' or 'have' denotes receiving support or a helping hand from a powerful person or entity. Requests for amparo are rooted in challenging experiences devotees have with law enforcement, prisons, courts, hospitals, and tax offices, as well as with the vicissitudes of informal and insecure livelihoods and the vulnerability of patronage politics (see Section 5). The prototypical Santa Muerte supplication is '*no me dejes desamparado*' (don't leave me unprotected). Unsurprisingly, the notion of amparo is also used in Mexican law. As a legal device that mediates between citizens and the state, an amparo allows citizens to request a court to temporarily postpone an allegedly unlawful act by public authority (Reich 2007).[21] In popular religion, the notion of (des)amparo conveys 'how the Santa Muerte cult is a space for thinking about who protects whom, and from what', in which protection implies postponing the final encounter with danger or death (Roush 2014: 130).

A sophisticated analysis of the emic notions and practices of (des)amparo and paro with the help of classic anthropological theories of exchange, gifting, and reciprocity has come up with a continuum of practices of exchange and reciprocity (Kristensen 2019; Lomnitz 2019). Generalized long-term reciprocity between devotees and the saint, typically cultivated at home altars, creates the unconditional familial faith, loyalty, and intimacy of devotees towards the saint nurturing amparo. Balanced reciprocity is typical of more utilitarian, and possibly more short-lived promise–favour exchanges between devotees and Santa Muerte, rather associated with *paros* (Kristensen 2011: 155; Perdigón 2008: 65). The fact that these different reciprocity dynamics intertwine in daily life explains why Santa Muerte may be epitomized as an unconditionally loving and helpful mother, as well as a castigating and even vengeful one. Interestingly, devotees may verbalize this paradox by normatively distinguishing between *devoción de corazón* (from the heart, deeply committed) and more transactional relationships.

A final theological component concerns the question as to whether successful interventions by Santa Muerte in human affairs should be classified as miracles. It has been argued that such interventions cannot comply with the definitional thresholds of miracles found in traditional canonical scriptures, such as the absence of a foundational miracle narrative. As noted, Santa Muerte petitionary rituals and intercessions reflect mundane rather than supernatural concerns. The cult's theological core is therefore best described with the notion of the (am)paro, rather than miracle (Bigliardi 2016: 317–18). Prominent cult leader Enriqueta Romero unambiguously supports this view, but for a different reason. Averse to theological connoisseurship, and in her typical colloquial style she responded to the question if devotees at her shrine request miracles from Santa Muerte: 'What do you think? Of course, they do, but La Flaca provides a 'paro', not miracles. Don't forget that to carry out miracles nothing more [is needed] than our almighty God. . . . Nor are we

---

[21] Amparos are often used by powerful political and economic interests to postpone or disrupt legal cases against them.

going to say God is equal to death. 'Diosito' works miracles for us and La Flaca tons of paros' (Alba Vega & Braig 2022: 559). However, the fact that ordinary people attribute, request, and use the notion of miracle in relation to Santa Muerte is recognized at the Congregación Nacional shrine in Ecatepec, where one of the central effigies is aptly called La Milagrosa. Acknowledging the ambiguity about miracles yet again underscores the critical role of meaning-making practices from below in shaping Santa Muerte religiosity.

4 The Organization and Politics of Santa Muerte Devotion

While the absence of a centrally sanctioned Santa Muerte canon and popular religion-making facilitated the cult's expressive and devotional diversity and dynamics, the latter also became the subject of organizational and political interventions. This section examines the emergence and major features of spiritual and organizational leadership since 2000. Soon after the cult started to expand and certain shrines attracted considerable followings, various spiritual leaders and ritual operators emerged, who propagated rules about the cult, communicated to them through Santa Muerte revelations. With this, the institutionalization of the cult began (García Zavala 2007: 184). As devotees identified with certain leaders and shrines, congregations were formed that subsequently established chapters or associations elsewhere.

Although domestic shrines remained crucial in daily Santa Muerte devotion, the expansion of public collective rituals spawned increasing organizational complexity and the crystallization of different and rivalling perspectives on theological matters, the governance of public gatherings, legal issues, economic affairs, and, of course, decision-making, and political authority. With leaders' different strategies to expand or consolidate their congregations came new interests, divisions, competition, and conflict.

This section argues that during the last quarter of a century the key organizational and political processes within the Santa Muerte community at large have revolved around negotiating institutional and spiritual centralization and more localized or autonomist approaches. Based on the examination of key leaderships and congregations, including the role of family, I show how the cult's entrenched decentralized practices informed its organizational and political makeup and reproduced spaces for sundry iconographic and spiritual input from below.

Emerging Leaders

At the beginning of the cult's formative years (ca. 2001–11), an array of spiritual leaders and guardians of popular shrines emerged. In time, some of these – such as the shaman Macario and Manuel Valadez – never formed their own congregations, but became Santa Muerte organic intellectuals who exerted considerable but indirect influence. Others had promising starts as spiritual leaders and/or shrine guardians, but soon faded away. I will focus on three key protagonists in the evolution of the cult in Mexico City and beyond: since the early 2000s, Santa Muerte leaders David Romo, Enriqueta Romero, and later the Legaria Vargas family, together with their most trusted collaborators, wielded much influence over the principles and practices of devotion.[22]

Initially, these and other leaders cooperated in different ways. At the end of 2001, David Romo led religious ceremonies at Enriqueta Romero's shrine, while the current leader of the Congregación Nacional de Santa Muerte in Ecatepec recognized the latter as the cult's pioneer and requested her godmotherly blessing for his first altar. Romo was also invited to celebrate mass in Ecatepec, and the first leader of the Santa Muerte Internacional, Jonathan Legaria Vargas, brought his followers to public manifestations organized by Romo (Kristensen 2019; Valverde 2020; Marín 2007). At the time, Romero herself offered services at private altars and prisons in Mexico City and nearby states (García Zavala 2007: 214; Alba Vega & Braig 2022: 568). The 'guardians', as they were often called, of public and private altars formed networks in Mexico City and beyond. A 2008 census of street ceremonies in Mexico City and Puebla found that a little over a third had connections to Romo's Iglesia Santa Católica Apostólica Tradicional, little less than a third to Enriqueta Romero's shrine on Alfarería street, while the last third were carried out independently by local devotees, albeit mainly copying the devotional practices developed by the first two (Kristensen 2019: 139).

Devotional expertise began to circulate and was adopted and adapted everywhere. However, theological and other discrepancies soon emerged among the most prominent leaders and their followings, and turned into open disagreements, rivalries, and conflicts. The growing number of Santa Muerte devotees, the mushrooming of public shrines, and the swelling of collective ceremonies prompted the assembling of congregational units, organizational structures, and networks, forging religious and political authority, and, finally, converting the latter into economic opportunities. Unsurprisingly, these developments resulted in divergent views, diverse projects, and conflicting ambitions.

'I have an altar that attracts many people, God knows why'

The shrine established in 2001 by Enriqueta Romero in Tepito made her the cult's most prominent and influential leader. She enjoys enormous spiritual and

---

[22] Kristensen (2019) estimates that the group of leaders and their closest collaborators that decisively molded devotion consists of no more than fifteen to twenty people.

social authority among devotees from the Mexico City metropolitan area but also from the states of Mexico, Puebla, Querétaro, Oaxaca, and beyond. Unlike most other street altars and shrines across Mexico, the one at Romero's house has no official name nor a registration with the state. It is commonly known as the Tepito or Alfafería Santa Muerte sanctuary. Over the years Romero became a much sought-after spokesperson by the national and international media, despite or perhaps because she was initially portrayed by those media as 'a diabolical, satanic woman, a witch' (Alba Vega & Braig 2022: 554). Helped by her down-to-earth personality and non-dogmatic theological views, Enriqueta and her collaborators profoundly shaped the stock of prayers and symbolic practices of Santa Muerte devotion, but they did so in an impromptu manner by 'doing' rather than by systemizing and encoding.

In 2016, she outlined her religious and moral views, which ultimately shaped the shrine's organizational and political dimensions, in her flowery Mexico City argot: 'We are here because of him [God], not because we are groovy', and 'Yes, I have an altar that attracts many people, God knows why' (Alba Vega & Braig 2022: 554–5). She has remained deeply committed to the family-run street altar that is open to devotees from all walks of life and to other popular religious beliefs and saints, such as Santería, Palo Mayombe, Saint Jude, the Virgin of Guadalupe, but also the devil, the latter of which explains the resentment of other leaders. She espouses a laissez-faire perspective on devotion: 'No, honey, there are no rules here, I am not into the Catholic mode. . . . Here everybody does what he or she fucking wants. What I want is faith and that you speak to *la muerte* from the heart and that you humbly put a request to her. Nothing else' (Alba Vega & Braig 2022: 567).

This doesn't mean that Enriqueta honors all requests. For example, she forcefully refuses to read mass or to carry out marriages and baptisms, common at other shrines: 'A mass? God help me. Don't fuck with me, that's what the churches and the priests are for, to do mass. How do you dare to read mass, you are nobody' (Alba Vega & Braig 2022: 555). And yet, she acknowledges the other's right to work the way they want with God's blessing. Her theological, social, and moral beliefs are deeply open-minded and individualistic. People are responsible for their own social and religious choices: 'You know what you are getting into. You are therefore not unaware, nobody pulled you into this, nor did anybody tell you to be a criminal. You like this business and you do it. . . . Here there is no "I didn't know"' (Alba Vega & Braig 2022: 557). This worldview epitomizes a longing for popular sovereignty and social and religious agency, which is antithetical to hierarchization and canonization. While Enriqueta Romero and her de facto congregation have shaped the institutionalization of Santa Muerte devotion, she never aspired any special position of power nor sought to capitalize politically on her recognized authority and visibility (Bigliardi 2016: 307; Quiroga 2011). The Tepito sanctuary is an extended family-run shrine, an unnamed de facto and essentially unregulated congregation – probably Mexico's largest – under the undisputed leadership of Enriqueta Romero that has abstained from establishing a particular Santa Muerte brand, assembling a formal organization, or founding branches elsewhere.

Building a Santa Muerte Cathedral?

Doña Queta's approach stands in stark contrast to the ambitious institution-building efforts by the controversial and boisterous self-appointed archbishop of the Santa Muerte church, David Romo, who in the 1990s founded the Iglesia Santa Católica Apostólica Tradicional México–USA (ISCAT MX-USA), a traditionalist pre-Second Vatican Council Catholic Church with roots in the nineteenth-century Old Catholic Church. Formed as a Catholic priest, the starting point of Romo's worldview and endeavours could not have been more different from Enriqueta Romero's. Romo originally started out in social work until he ran out of funds, after which he founded ISCAT (Chesnut 2012: 42). His interest in Santa Muerte thus developed from *within* a new and not officially recognized Catholic Church. He claimed evidence in the Holy Scriptures of the compatibility between Christian theology and Santa Muerte devotion, declared the 'sanctity of death', and tapped into the potential of the latter to attract people from the margins of society to the house of God (García Zavala 2007: 187–94). He allowed devotees to place Santa Muerte effigies and perform rituals in his church – only a few blocks away from Romero's shrine – mentioned the saint in mass, rewrote prayers, and reframed her image from an entity associated with 'destruction and suffering' to a more virtuous one (Kristensen 2019: 142). Romo also promoted networking by circulating six pilgrim Santa Muerte images at temporary host families, a practice soon replicated elsewhere (Leija Parra 2010).

As the congregation grew, Romo put together a team of trusted collaborators (*mayordomos*), an important step in his incipient organization. In 2003, with the new law governing Mexican state–church relations in hand, Romo's ISCAT obtained official state recognition. On the 15 August that year, which was decreed the patron saint's day, Archbishop Romo and thousands of devotees celebrated the incorporation of Santa Muerte in the church's theological tenets (García Zavala 2007: 193). Even today, shrines in Mexico once associated with David Romo's organization commemorate this date with fiestas and processions. For example, for the guardian of the Iglesia de Santa Muerte y Barbara

Bendita in downtown Puebla, established in 2008, the 'day we were reborn' symbolizes the successful collective struggle for the cult's recognition.[23]

Romo displayed a range of initiatives to expand the cult, to strengthen his leadership, and to be at the forefront of its institutionalization (Chesnut 2012b: 41). Through his public declarations and manifestations, he strove to position himself as the main spokesperson of the growing Santa Muerte community. He started to charge devotees for religious services, allegedly to fund constructing a Santa Muerte cathedral, the would-be central shrine of the burgeoning cult. This ended the short-lived cooperation between Romo and Romero. The controversy about profiting from Santa Muerte devotion lingered on for years, with Romo symbolizing the dishonorable priest (De la Fuente 2016: 177; Kristensen 2019: 138). The institutionalizing and centralizing ambitions were most apparent in Romo's efforts to erect other shrines and altars or become associated with them. He also invested in training a new generation of priests in Mexico City and elsewhere and managed a team of delegates. For years, he exerted a strong influence over local spiritual leaders, their shrines, and devotees. Argyriades (2014) has shown how rivalling local Santa Muerte leaders in Veracruz fought each other to control the popular religious market and therefore sought strategic alliances with Romo and his delegates. At the same time, the deepening hostility between Romo and Romero in Mexico City exacerbated rivalries between local charismatic leaders and their followers.

Romo's organization also became involved with the Parroquia del Señor de la Misericordia y la Santa Muerte in the city of Chetumal. He led the first mass at the shrine and ordained deacons during subsequent visits (Higuera Bonfil 2015a). During several years an ISCAT envoy read mass monthly at a shrine in Guadalajara, and was also active in Veracruz and Puebla (Bravo Lara 2013; Del Bornio 2008). A shrine in Puebla obtained an effigy called La Milagrosa from Romo's Mexico City sanctuary, after which he attempted to incorporate the shrine into his network. Keen on maintaining their independence the Puebla guardians refused.

While the media-savvy Romo appeared to be on his way to build a national Santa Muerte stronghold, not least by negotiating alliances with congregations outside Mexico City, countervailing forces were in the making. By 2011, Romo's centralizing strategy had failed. After only two years, ISCAT lost its official registration following a complaint by one of the church's own priests who resented Romo's adoption of Santa Muerte as a deviation from the statutes (Garcés Marrero 2020: 15). Romo criticized the government's decision as repression of the Santa Muerte cult instigated by the Roman Catholic Church.

---

[23] Interview with Emilia, Puebla, 4 August 2023.

He mobilized thousands of devotees to defend their civil and religious rights, while relations with the Roman Catholic Church quickly deteriorated. In 2009, he urged his followers not to vote for the party in power. Since the church registration was never restored, Romo was unable to raise funds or own church properties, which thwarted his organizational and leadership ambitions (Chesnut 2012b: 45).

While focused on external adversaries, Romo had made enemies within his own congregation, and the Santa Muerte community. He was widely viewed a 'megalomaniac', as someone with 'caudillo' aspirations to centralize and institutionalize Santa Muerte devotion. He was criticized for economic profiteering, and accused of embezzlement, womanizing, and criticizing leaders of rival shrines, who refused to consider him the 'true leader of the cult' and instead favoured unmediated exchanges between devotees and their preferred Santa Muerte (Martín 2014: 206–7). It has been suggested that losing registration prompted Romo to remove the skeletal effigies from his church, perhaps hoping the authorities might reconsider their decision, and replace her with a slick, incarnated, and winged 'Angel of Death' effigy, pointedly pictured as a 'department store mannequin with a scythe' (Garcés Marrero 2020: 19; Roush 2014: 137). However, in the church's own account the decision was driven by an incident during the spring of 2007 when the bodies of three murdered people were found in front of a Santa Muerte altar in a northern city as if it represented an offering (Bello n.d.). It caused consternation in the media and put Santa Muerte devotion in a suspicious light.

In any case, devotees found that the 'Angel of Death' resembled Romo's wife and categorically rejected the iconographic innovation. In their eyes the skeletal countenance continued to constitute the essence of Santa Muerte. Members of Romo's inner circle of priests and mayordomos left the church and established their own centres of worship, taking beloved images and devotees with them. For many the church had lost most of its influence, credibility, and legitimacy due to the arrogance and authoritarianism of its leader, who proved unwilling to respect popular devotional practices and sought to impose a project of centralized institutionalization (Fragoso 2007a: 130). Others resented his failure as a moral person and a trustworthy Catholic priest (Kristensen 2019: 151–2). Outside Romo's inner circle, the crisis caused twenty-five guardians of Santa Muerte altars to form the Congregación Nacional de la Santa Muerte in open opposition to Romo (Valverde 2020).

An existing network called Altares Unidos with around thirty leaders and their congregations from Mexico City and neighbouring states advocated the anti-hierarchical view that Santa Muerte didn't 'belong' to anybody (De la Fuente 2016: 178). The magazine *Devoción a La Santa Muerte* disseminated the view that privileged the devotional practices of ordinary people and their home altars above those of aspiring 'professional' religious specialists (Kristensen 2019: 141). David Romo had misread the critical importance of Santa Muerte religion-making from below and the distrust of ecclesiastical authority, political centralization, and theological glorification. In 2011, when little remained of his erstwhile influence, Romo was arrested and charged with kidnapping and money laundering (Proceso 2011). A year later, he was convicted and imprisoned. His attempt at institutional and spiritual centralization had utterly failed.

All in the Family

Some form of megalomania could also describe Jonathan Legaria Vargas, the founder and first leader of a shrine and congregation called Santa Muerte Internacional (SMI). Established in 2007, in Tultitlán to the north of Mexico City, the shrine features a twenty-two-metre-high Santa Muerte statue. A fascinating chiaroscuro figure, Legaria Vargas, who was better known as Comandante Pantera, had forged a social and religious leadership from rough and intense life experiences, which included poverty, drugs, gang violence, and prison. He cultivated the image of a self-made young man, who fended for himself and earned respect. Still in his twenties, he consciously crafted a life narrative in two booklets (both published in 2007) that sought to legitimize his leadership. *El hijo de la Santa Muerte*, which Higuera Bonfil (2022: 274) fittingly labelled a mythical tale allegedly penned by a journalist, portrays Legaria's experiences as a federal police officer, professional wrestler, leader of a motor club, as well as his excursions into Santería and Santa Muerte devotion during stays in Haiti and Africa (Marín 2007). In *Santa Muerte revelaciones* he outlined ideas about life and devotion, one being the ruthlessly pragmatic call for happiness: 'not in heaven, but with ours in the worldly here, not in the divine when we are already dead' (quoted in Higuera Bonfil 2022: 275). In theological terms, Santa Muerte was framed by her close relationships with African religious practices and artefacts. He also put together a team of collaborators to manage the shrine in Tultitlán and disseminate the cult. Thus, in a brief period, Legaria Vargas made clear his intentions of institutionalizing the SMI and laid the foundations for leadership, organizational structures, and devotional rituals. He was, however, prevented from capitalizing on these steps because in July 2008 Jonathan Legaria Vargas was assassinated in a hail of bullets.[24]

---

[24] There were rumours about a criminal settlement, but others claimed that Legaria's public statements had angered vested interests (Casal Sáenz 2016: 91–6; Kingsbury 2021a).

After the tragic incident, his mother, Enriqueta Vargas, who had until then not engaged in the cult, assumed leadership of the nascent organization and congregation. She soon took it upon herself to consolidate and expand SMI through a flurry of initiatives and innovations, simultaneously stressing her son's spirit and legacy (Higuera Bonfil 2022). In time, the symbolic position of Comandante Pantera gradually acquired saintly features as intercessor, and his image started to pop up at SMI altars. Currently, the main Tultitlán shrine holds a prominent Pantera effigy, a kind of 'adjunct folk saint of Santa Muerte' (Bigliardi 2015/2016; Kingsbury 2021a) (Figure 8).

Vargas adapted rituals, introduced new prayers, songs, and iconographic aspects – she was fond of pre-Hispanic outfits and artefacts – and finalized the congregation's ten ordinances previously outlined by her son. She disseminated the cult through social media, another booklet, and a film project. She successfully filed requests for intellectual property rights over prayers and a logo, initiated the procedure to secure the congregation's legal status, and improved SMI's administrative and financial management. Finally, although she was particularly committed to social work for the sick and prisoners, her most important contribution lay in promoting the territorial expansion of the SMI. She was an excellent networker who appointed regional representatives

Figure 8 Comandante Pantera effigy at the Tultitlán shrine. Photo by author.

responsible for recruiting devotees and looking after them. Enriqueta Vargas invested time and resources in visiting regional chapters, which paid dividends in terms of her political and devotional authority. With a considerable group of around thirty local and regional SMI representatives and shrines in Mexico and the United States, she formed the so-called *Gran Alianza*, which served as a conduit for the development of a SMI liturgical and devotional identity.

Unlike David Romo's failed attempt at national expansion and centralized control, Enriqueta Vargas's inclusive networking strategy brought together leaders and shrines with distinctive histories and features and kept the cult open to diverse devotional traditions if they didn't conflict with SMI's central beliefs. Without experiencing impositions or major changes in local ways of worshipping, it gave way to constructing 'Tultitlán as a coordinating instance' only (Higuera Bonfil 2022: 285). In other words, while institutionalization of the SMI congregation was obvious, it avoided the pitfalls of centralization. In contrast to Romo's caudillo ambitions, Enriqueta Vargas' undisputed leadership and authority accommodated difference. Coordination allowed grassroots devotional agency.

At the end of 2018, with a firmly consolidated SMI in place, Enriqueta Vargas passed away. The organization's administrative body handed the leadership position to Enriqueta's twenty-nine-year-old daughter Kristel Legaria Vargas, Jonathan's sister. After little more than a decade since its founding and conscious of its symbolic and political capital, the SMI had interiorized succession within the family as an expedient mechanism. In the summer of 2023, Kristel Legaria, an amiable corporate lawyer dressed in jeans and a leather jacket and wearing a massive necklace made of black and purple beads and white skulls, showed me around the SMI complex in Tultitlán. One shrine especially conveyed the intimate connections forged between SMI devotion and the Legaria Vargas family: it holds, among other things, an 'Aztec' garment used by Enriqueta during services and a large Santa Muerte effigy dressed in white called *La Santa Viva*, once part of Comandante Pantera's private altar. When I inquired about the enigmatic 'living Santa Muerte' moniker, Kristel told me that when taking the statue out of her brother's house it turned out to be extremely heavy and 'warm', almost unmovable, as if it was alive and resisted the transfer.[25]

Personalism and Diversity

The examination of the organizational and political features and trajectories of Enriqueta Romero's Tepito altar, Romo's ISCAT, and SMI highlights the

---

[25] Interview with Kristel, Tultitlán, 30 July 2023.

essential role of personal leadership and family relations. Similar processes have been observed elsewhere at smaller shrines (De la Fuente 2013). Personalistic networks and loyalties have long characterized Latin American social and political organizations, and new religious movements or organizations are no exception. In the same vein, one would expect popular religious organizations not to be immune to factionalism, clientelism, and bossism. As indicated, factional disputes in the Mexico City Santa Muerte community migrated to other parts of the country. The interweaving of devotion and extended familial centres of worship has diverse effects. Familial devotional units come with intimacy, but often also generate conflicts and rivalries. Many trusted personal and quasi-familial relationships and networks within congregations have ended in divisions and schisms (Kristensen 2019). Since personalistic or charismatic leaders shape devotional formats and practices and intrinsically contest centralized institutionalization and strict devotional regulation, they are also partially responsible for the cult's vitality and decentralized diversity.

The complex interactions between leadership aims and popular agency and the dialectic of doctrine and division indeed account for much of the cult's vitality and diversity (Pansters 2019: 39). In the process of becoming a visible and sizeable religious phenomenon, Santa Muerte morphed into an all-purpose saint. Petitions for protection and support in many real-life domains in exchange for offerings and faith have found expression in the diversification of material forms and functions. Symbolic and aesthetic mutations are discernible in distinctive theological framings, devotional practices, and articulations with other saints and popular religions (Flores Martos 2019; Garcés Marrero 2021). The conversion of two-dimensional Santa Muerte representations into countless three-dimensional forms and designs reconstituted the cult, humanizing the saint and endowing her with both familial intimacy and effective agency. Digital dissemination multiplied the cult's reach and impact, increasing its visibility and variation. All of these developments have generated increasing organizational and political complexities and contradictions and demonstrate how diverse Santa Muerte devotion and religious agency have challenged projects of institutionalized centralization and canonization.

5 Santa Muerte Devotion and Society: Vulnerability, Insecurity, and the Roman Catholic Church

While Santa Muerte devotion is shaped by a long history of miraculous images and folk saints, its extraordinary iconographic and religious allure, and its theological peculiarities – sanctification of death, the (*des*)*amparo* complex – grant it a unique position in the current popular religious landscape. What explains its notable emergence and expansion since the turn of the twenty-first century? Some ideas have been put forward. The spontaneous decision to place an effigy in a public space in 2001 triggered a cause-and-effect process of offerings, the birth of street altars, spreading devotion, more altars, media attention, and so on. The rise in Santa Muerte devotion can also be viewed through the prism of the escalation of drug-related violence. Disregarding the social basis of votive practices, a rather ingenuous explanation pointed at the effectiveness of saintly miracles. I will argue that these circumstances and others may all play a role in the rise of a complex social, cultural, and religious phenomenon such as the Santa Muerte cult. Anthropological research about new religious and spiritual phenomena indicates the diverse ways in which ordinary people living under conditions of neoliberal capitalism, state abandonment, and inequalities and violence seek protection and support from alternative sources, such as Santa Muerte. In vulnerable and precarious livelihoods, individuals and families must deal with bread-and-butter issues (employment, social mobility), deficient public services (education and health, including the COVID-19 pandemic), an arbitrary legal system, as well as crime, insecurity, and violence.

Studying how broader societal processes, practices, and institutions shape Santa Muerte devotion merits specific attention to the Roman Catholic Church, which maintains an official position that rejects and repudiates instances of what is deemed to be idolatrous superstition. The tense relationship between the Roman Catholic Church and the Santa Muerte community is further complicated by the fact that the latter harbors stigmatized vulnerable groups such as prostitutes, homosexuals, drug addicts, undocumented migrants, and convicts, who feel unwelcome in the Catholic Church. The result is an incommensurability between the proximity of lived Santa Muerte commitment to popular Catholicism and the hostile stance of the Catholic hierarchy.

Answering the main question of this section requires an examination of the social conditions, forces, and institutions that shape the livelihoods of ordinary Mexicans. I subsequently look at socio-economic circumstances marked by exclusion and vulnerability, and the proliferation of insecurity, violence, and impunity.

Understanding Vulnerability and Protections

Histories of Mexico's idiosyncratic popular religious practices and movements have always been associated with shifting political economies, ethnic relations, political regimes, and cultural repertoires (Hughes 2021; Pescador 2009; Smith 2019). Rubin, Smilde, & Junge (2014) employed the concepts of lived citizenship and lived religion – emphasizing situated daily practices and meanings – to explore the interconnections among religion, citizenship, politics, security, and economy in contemporary Latin America. Within this framework, popular religion 'can provide meaning to situations and empower agency', particularly in zones of multiple crises where needs are unmet and survival itself threatened (Rubin et al. 2014: 16). Agency can assume the form of resistance against oppressive authorities, as in carceral institutions (Yllescas 2016).

This perspective resonates with the findings of comparative research about novel forms of enchantment, religion, witchcraft, and 'occult economies' in the context of millennial capitalism and violent democracies. Occult-related or new religious practices feature an intrusion into the public sphere, while ordinary people perceive their predicament as caused by mysterious forces that generate value and wealth and corrode communitarian protections (Comaroff & Comaroff 2001). This makes clear 'why the ethical dimensions of occult economies ... often express themselves in religious movements that pursue instant material returns and yet condemn those who enrich themselves in non-traditional ways' (Comaroff & Comaroff 2001: 25–6). The parallels with Santa Muerte's problem-solving and 'equalizing' capacity are evident. In the Latin American context, Santa Muerte devotion is rooted in histories of folk Catholicism, but it is also part of the growing prominence and visibility of miraculous folk saints who 'condense and incarnate death as an agent with the power to intervene in the daily reality' (Flores Martos 2019: 86). The study of several of these folk saints, for example Botitas Negras in Chile and the Argentinean San La Muerte, has indicated that the interactions between devotees and popular saints supplant the functions of an absent state.[26]

Fragoso (2007b) was one of the first to explore the correlations between 'social vulnerability' and new popular religiosities in Mexico. Closely related to poverty and marginalization, vulnerability and precarity emphasize people's risks and uncertainties due to ineffective social protections in work, healthcare, and education. Has the saint then become 'a talisman against the risks of everyday life' (Hernández Hernández 2011: 39)? Deficient social protections translate into experiences of disjunctive citizenship, in which civil, political, and social rights ostensibly guaranteed by the state are severely compromised by inequalities and exclusion. Many find themselves in the informal economy or the worst-paid layers of formal employment. Economic precarity easily bleeds into informal housing. The recent emergence of the Santa Muerte cult in the

---

[26] For a comparative analysis of the considerably less sizeable San La Muerte cult and Santa Muerte, see Yllescas (2023). See also Graziano (2007: 77–111).

historical epicentre of Mexico City's shadow economy is hardly a coincidence (Huffschmid 2019; Konove 2018).

As citizens grapple with vulnerable, precarious, and unstable conditions, Santa Muerte devotion creates an alternative order, or nomos (Fragoso 2007b: 32). The saint 'is invoked for protection and strength, in the hope of transforming disorder into order' (Oleszkiewicz-Peralba 2015:116). From a human rights perspective, the state's failure as a guarantor of rights has damaged the social fabric and fostered anomie. But rather than seeing Santa Muerte as an entity at the 'intersection of hybrid religiosity and existential desperation, a near nihilism wrought by macropolitics of the nation-state', for devotees the saint represents an alternative and hope-generating agent that counteracts anomie and 'knits the broken threads into a new texture' (Castells Ballarín 2008: 20; Ramírez 2009: 76).

To grasp the connections between social structure and popular religion, Müller (2021) has developed a typology of 'milieu experiences' of social and economic risks. The 'experience of weak social ties' focuses on the elementary level of households and families, and indirectly on markets and the state. For example, Fernanda – a young woman with a history of disrupted families, sexual violence, and domestic violence – learned to fend for herself and her children. Without family support, contacts, or access to state institutions, they were on their own. In her view, Santa Muerte has protected her from life-threatening situations and prevented her children being taken away. She considers the saint 'a mother', an agentive entity with whom she chats, eats, smokes, and drinks, and with whom she formed an alternative and stable family-like relationship (Müller 2021: 137–73).

Health issues are frequently mentioned by devotees as motivations to resort to Santa Muerte. In Mexico City, Juan Antonio had a near-death experience after a stabbing incident. Although he was ready to die, Santa Muerte – an 'Angel of God' – intervened and gave him another chance in this world.[27] A substantial part of the letters sent to the *Doy gracias* section of the *Devoción a la Santa Muerte* magazine concerns health issues. Considering the seriousness of the COVID-19 pandemic, it is worth reflecting on its impact on the cult. With around 333,000 deaths (as of October 2023) and, after Peru, the highest observed case-to-fatality ratio in the world, Mexico was particularly hard hit by the pandemic.[28] These numbers justify asking if the risks of COVID-19 infection, serious illness, negative economic fallout, and death drove the country's vulnerable population towards Santa Muerte for protection.

---

[27] Interview with Juan Antonio, Mexico City, 27 July 2022.
[28] In absolute numbers of deaths, Mexico came after the United States, Brazil, India, and Russia. Johns Hopkins Coronavirus Resource Center, https://coronavirus.jhu.edu/data/mortality, accessed 20 February 2024.

After the pandemic had receded, I discussed the matter with devotees and owners of shrines and esoteric shops across Mexico. When the country went into crisis mode it had immediate consequences: while street altars often remained open for individual visits, collective gatherings and rosaries were suspended. Esoteric shops in markets closed. Views from shrine owners diverged. Some had doubts about the virus itself and distrusted government measures. For them, the pandemic changed little: when it came to protection and well-being, they had always trusted Santa Muerte more than government institutions. Supplicating the saint in these circumstances can be read as social or political critique. Others subscribed and adhered to official regulations, moving all devotional activities online. The Santa Muerte Internacional shrine, for example, maintained strict guidelines about face masks, social distancing, and controlled access after it reopened in July 2020 (Garcés Marrero 2021: 84; Higuera Bonfil 2022: 292). As expected, those already involved in the cult responded to the risks and ancillary effects of the virus by entreating Santa Muerte for protection and healing. Special Coronavirus candles and prayers started to circulate. A boutique owner sprinkled Santa Muerte lotion on the threshold to prevent COVID-19 from entering (Kingsbury 2021b). At one shrine in Mexico City, a Santa Muerte effigy itself wore a facemask (Garcés Marrero 2021). Nowadays, the SMI complex in Tultitlán holds a large mural entitled 'Santa Muerte del COVID', painted in pre-Hispanic motifs with a Maya pyramid, a feathered skeletal warrior, and images of the cult's defunct leaders, and a list of names of people who died during the pandemic. Although Santa Muerte devotion mediated the COVID-19 pandemic and affected its practices in numerous ways, there is no evidence that it did so in significant ways: there was no large influx of new devotees nor a sharp increase in Santa Muerte paraphernalia sales. Compared to the intense experience of an existential health crisis elsewhere in the world, and despite the relatively high death toll, for many among Mexico's disenfranchised social groups the COVID-19 pandemic was one more of many serious livelihood challenges. A community leader in one of the toughest parts of the Guadalajara metropolitan area told me that people were aware of the pandemic, 'but within their reality, they didn't give a shit'.[29]

Insecurity, Violence, and Crime

The vulnerability and precarity experienced by lower-class citizens extend beyond the uncertainties of informal employment, ineffective state protections, or broken households, and encompass a dysfunctional rule of law and impunity, for which they seek solutions.

---

[29] Interview with Vicente, Tlajomulco de Zúñiga, 1 August 2022.

In dealing with 'the precariousness of their trade and the contingent nature of their rights', street vendors and informal businesses, for instance, face rent-seeking extortion by administrative authorities or the police (Konove 2018: 10). Forced into corrupt financial transactions, individuals find legal protection inaccessible. If the law has been a tool of political and economic subjugation, it also exempts the powerful. In this context, Santa Muerte appears as an independent and reliable *justo juez* (just judge).

The contingent application of the law is a daily reality and a philosophical contradiction deeply engrained in Latin America's social and political institutions. This applies to many, but in particular to those who eke out a living on society's fringes, such as sex workers, petty criminals, or taxi drivers working unsafe barrios. Prisoners arguably find themselves in the least protected conditions: contending with arbitrary prison guards, corrupt lawyers and judges, violence, inadequate healthcare and nourishment, they rely almost entirely on external resources and protection, and some must even manage without these. In addition to experiencing the mutilation of the self – often literally – upon entering the total institution of the prison, inmates inhabit a world beyond constitutional rights, legal protections, and the prison's own regulations, according to Yllescas' (2018) ethnographic research. Everything has a price – from a space to sleep, the right to walk the corridors, and acceptable food, to opportunities to participate in social programs, or to generate an income by selling sweets, handicrafts, telephone cards, services, or drugs. Governed by para-institutional coercive rule, inmates resort to entities from the religious 'gray zone', such as Santa Muerte, who both protect against existential dangers and safeguard illicit activities. Many had been familiar with the cult since childhood or adolescent street life, others since in prison, often in combination with Santería or Satanism. Sporting a Santa Muerte tattoo may prevent physical violence, lending the saint a sovereign quality in a social world governed by precarity and contingent rights.

Driven by economic hardships and criminal violence and subjected to stringent securitization, migrants from Mexico, Central and South America and beyond, make their way to the Mexico–US borderlands – spaces of exception 'where an individual's rights and protections under law can be stripped away upon entrance' (De León 2015: 27; Martín 2014). Migration and the border region have played an important role in the transnational presence of Santa Muerte devotion, a fascinating example of which is the return migration of an effigy from California to Mexico, where its owner, who had migrated to the United States years before, founded a new congregation (Calvo-Quirós 2022: 247; Thompson 1998). Central American migrants (and smugglers) request the blessing of Santa

Muerte before continuing their hazardous journey north on top of the infamous cargo train known as *La Bestia* (De León 2024: 98; González Velázquez et al. 2019). Discussing their social and legal precarity on the other side, De León (2015) mentions numerous migrants who, after years working and building families in the United States, were suddenly deported after a minor offence, pushing them back into the deadly zone of exception. The social conditions of devotees from Mexican migrant communities in the United States share similarities with their peers in Mexico. Los Angeles and New York shrines welcome vulnerable people as ex-convicts, sex workers, addicts, trans persons, and homosexuals. Undocumented migrants seek spiritual support to face economic precarity, legal uncertainty, and encounters with US law enforcement. Legalized migrants may live from paycheck to paycheck, and battle with family, health, employment, and romantic issues (Graf 2023; Higuera Bonfil 2016; Müller 2021).

In addition to the tapestry of socio-economic, political, and cultural vulnerabilities, a remarkable surge in violence and insecurity has swept through Mexico, initially spurred by the economic and political crises of the mid-1990s, then exacerbated by the escalation and territorial expansion of criminal violence, massive militarization, and armed non-state defense forces (Pansters 2015; Pansters et al. 2018; Pansters & Serrano 2023). Since 2006, the destructive dynamics of drug trafficking, the diversification of organized crime rooted in territorial control, along with militarized state interventions have resulted in hundreds of thousands of fatalities and disappearances and a climate of impunity affecting the lives of millions of Mexicans.

It is important to point out that the social origins of vulnerability and precarity, as well as the subsequent quest for alternative sources of authority, order, and protection, precede and transcend the surge in violence and insecurity directly linked to the global war on drugs. Viewing Santa Muerte devotion solely as an epiphenomenon of neoliberal capitalism (the 'saint of NAFTA') or of drug-related violence and death, or even as a practice that 'promotes violence and cultivates insurrection', is overly simplistic (Bowden 2006; Cervantes 2011: 27). It is just as deeply entrenched in popular Catholic devotional culture. Nonetheless, it is equally implausible to see the growth of the cult disconnected from neoliberal restructuring, state abandonment, deepening inequalities, and economic crises. Likewise, if it is abundantly clear that Santa Muerte is 'not just a narco-saint', the drug trafficking–violence–militarization complex has so deeply affected all societal domains that its relevance for Santa Muerte devotion is inevitable (Kingsbury & Chesnut 2020). Flores Martos (2019) has pointed at the correlation between the rise in violent deaths and the expansion of the Santa Muerte cult. Chilling and reliable testimonies have emerged about cruel Santa Muerte rituals inside some branches of Mexico's most notorious criminal organizations (Gallardo 2022; García Reyes 2021). Altars found in hideouts and safehouses belonging to organized crime made headlines (Lomnitz 2005: 492; Roush 2014). The administrator of a shrine in Ciudad Juárez told me that during the heyday of the city's security crisis (2009–2012), drug traffickers, sicarios (hitmen), and corrupt police officers had frequented the place. The shrine was shot at, and one devotee was murdered after he left. Another shrine was burnt down.[30] In 2009, the Mexican military destroyed dozens of shrines in the northeastern region around Nuevo Laredo and Reynosa (Loya 2009).

Finally, the impact of drug-related insecurity, corruption, and violence is perhaps most clearly seen in the deepening of historically existing opaque arrangements between state and non-state actors, legal and illegal practices, and formal and informal institutions. These arrangements give rise to a gray area for inherently risky transactions between criminals, police officers, politicians, and business people, who are therefore in constant need of overlords, or sovereigns, that guarantee protection, albeit temporarily (Pansters 2018).[31] It is an environment in which the state and the law coalesce with informal or illegal agents, and in which Santa Muerte is consulted by all. Just as one may encounter migrants, drug traffickers, and police officers at the shrine of Jesús Malverde in Culiacán, Sinaloa, it is common to see market women, (petty) criminals, and law enforcement agents mingle at Santa Muerte altars. The reason is simple: the gray zone is unstable, precarious, and dangerous.

Santa Muerte and the Roman Catholic Church

The emergence of Santa Muerte as a burgeoning urban form of religiosity highlights how devotees employ visual, performative, and spatial practices to confront existential uncertainties. The significance of visual elements in public spaces contributes to the cult's place-making qualities through the appropriation and sacralization of secular spaces and the establishment of new religious focal points. Because they demand recognition and social justice, new popular religious movements require visibility, often involving 'the inversion of the religious world' through the ex- and reappropriation of traditional religious meanings (Villamil Uriarte & Cisneros 2011). This ties into the perspective that in a postsecular world, religion is no longer considered a leftover from the past and that its entanglement with secular claims of social justice and political

---

[30] Interview with Diego, 30 July 2016, Ciudad Juárez.
[31] Several shrine owners talked about prominent politicians and top-level law enforcement agents covertly devoted to Santa Muerte, information that cannot be verified.

emancipation explains how people handle the contradictions of Latin America's multiple modernities (Rubin et al. 2014: 9). As a mediator between religiosity and everyday life, Santa Muerte should also be placed in the context of Catholicism's recent past. During the 1970s, in Mexico City's poor neighbourhoods and elsewhere, Catholic liberation theology deliberately forged connections with marginalized groups. Over time, however, just as the state abandoned its developmental aspirations and corporatist coalitions, the Catholic Church hierarchy has moved away from the doctrine of the 'preferential option for the poor' (Huffschmid 2019).

Many devotees see themselves as having drifted away from Catholic religiosity and the institutional church. Some use the notion of alienation, while others take a politicized stance because of the sexual abuse scandals. Santa Muerte devotees often mention that they welcome people from all walks of life, including prostitutes, sexual minorities, jailbirds, and addicts, who habitually experience rejection and stigmatization by the church. While Santa Muerte devotion is associated with tolerance, inclusion, and nearness to ordinary people's lives and concerns, the church is deemed doctrinaire, exclusive, and distant.

This perception is reinforced by Catholic spokespersons voicing concerns, criticism, and outright rejection of the cult.[32] For instance, in 2011, to instruct pastoral workers, the Apóstoles de la Palabra missionary movement distributed 50,000 copies of the third edition of a booklet on Santa Muerte and other 'superstitions'. The movement's main objective was 'to strengthen the faith of Catholics in the face of the onslaught of sects and new religiosities'.[33] Authored by Zarazúa Campa, the booklet argued that the pursuit of material over spiritual development has led to a fertile ground for popular religiosities as Santa Muerte and other non-canonical saints. Santa Muerte devotion is portrayed as idolatry that exploits the vulnerabilities of the uneducated and needy, who mistakenly associate it with folk Catholicism. Such misconceptions necessitate correction through earnest Catholic missionary work. Theological arguments are marshalled against the cult: it is superstitious because devotees erroneously believe Santa Muerte images possess a power derived from certain rituals of consecration; it is idolatrous because devotees worship something that cannot establish a relationship with God. Since death is the cessation of life, Santa Muerte cannot help anybody, since 'she does not exist' (Fragoso 2007b: 14; Zarazúa Campa 2011: 46). In addition, Santa Muerte seems to be conflated with the Catholic notion of *muerte santa* (blessed death), which is dependent on a pious life.

---

[32] The following empirical information draws on Pansters (2019: 47–8).

[33] See www.apostolesdelapalabra.org/familia-misionera/movimiento-eclesial/, accessed 25 March 2020.

According to the booklet, once inside the cult some promote Satanism, while others legitimize crime and drug trafficking. It also asserts that Catholic priests specializing in exorcism have treated people involved in Santa Muerte devotion (2011: 42). In 2013, it was reported that 'the rising demand for exorcism' is partly explained by the increasing numbers of Mexicans joining the cult (Hernandez 2013). Setting aside theological considerations, Zarazúa Campa addresses the social dimensions of the cult, acknowledging 'the current socio-economic context, characterized by insecurity, unemployment, loss of purchasing power, and multiple problems in interpersonal relations' (2011: 60–1). Even so, the expansion of the cult is attributed to religious entrepreneurs who profit from selling services and devotional paraphernalia. Overall, the Apósteles de la Palabra booklet and other church publications and declarations consistently portrayed the Santa Muerte cult as an idolatrous superstition that capitalizes on the hardships of uninformed people, who are or may become entrapped in the world of crime, drug trafficking, and violence.

Opposition to the cult by the Catholic clergy goes back to the cult's early public appearances around the turn of the twenty-first century. In 1998, a conflict arose around a Santa Muerte chapel in Santa Ana Chapitiro, in the state of Michoacán, when local devotees clashed with the village priest. Soon, higher-ranking church officials from the archdiocese condemned the cult, declaring it a 'grave sin of superstition' (Vargas González 2004: 108). Other priests expressed disagreement, anger, and sarcasm (Perdigón 2008: 75). As the cult gained momentum nationwide and David Romo engaged in proselytizing and street protests in Mexico City, the church's upper hierarchy became actively involved. In May 2013, Cardinal Gianfranco Ravasi, president of the Vatican's Pontifical Council for Culture, publicly denounced the cult: 'Religion celebrates life, but here you have death. . . . It's not religion just because it's dressed up like religion; it's a blasphemy against religion.' Rome's envoi also highlighted the cult's alleged ties to drug cartels (Vatican Declares 2013). Subsequently, the Conferencia del Episcopado Mexicano (2013) dismissed the cult's purported social roots and suggested: '[B]ehind it is a kingdom of evil and people can become a victim of diabolical possession.'[34] In 2016, during his visit to Mexico, Pope Francis expressed his concerns about all those who 'seduced by the empty power of the world, praise illusions and embrace their macabre symbols to commercialize death in exchange for money. . . . I urge you not to underestimate the moral and antisocial challenge which the drug trade represents for Mexican society . . . as well as for the Church' (Pope Francis 2016). In general, the

---

[34] In terms of Knight's (2008: 250) Catholic Church's moral tripartite categorization, Santa Muerte would definitely be placed in the dangerous 'heresy/diabolism' section, not in the 'acceptable cult of saints' section.

negative and sometimes openly hostile views voiced by Catholic ecclesiastical authorities have found their way to social media platforms, where devotees have experienced discrimination by Catholic users (Gervasi 2018; Pérez Salazar & Gervasi 2015).

Despite all this, many Santa Muerte devotees – likely the overwhelming majority – continue to identify as Catholics. While some do so out of conviction, most are traditional or 'cradle Catholic' believers. Key features of the cult's devotional rituals are steeped in Catholic votive traditions. However, the theological and ritual proximity to popular Catholicism felt and professed by many Santa Muerte devotees – admittedly on their terms – is clearly at odds with the ecclesiastical hierarchy's unequivocal theological disapproval of the cult. It seems that while religious diversity is an undisputed social reality in contemporary Mexico, religious pluralism as a normative imperative and an ordinary virtue is not (Beckford 2008: 73–81).

Epilogue

Since the mid-1990s, Santa Muerte has evolved from a hidden and private object of worship to a publicly lived, increasingly extensive, and, above all, dynamic folk devotion. Facing social vulnerabilities, violence, and the contingent access to citizenship rights, ordinary people in Mexico and elsewhere need, as Lou Reed once sang, 'a busload of faith to get by'. They claim and cultivate manifold transcendental entities for support and protection. In a social and religious landscape featuring diversity, secularization, weakening institutional Roman Catholicism, new legal frameworks, and heterodox articulations, Santa Muerte has established herself as a powerful yet intimate saint. In essence, Santa Muerte devotion is about a personalized sense of faith, religiosity, and ritual votive practices that give meaning to, and help secure, a good life by transforming the devotees' lived environment and the world at large.

Opportunities for the personalization and individuation of Santa Muerte devotion abound: from the creation of private altars, the choice of effigies, adornments, offerings, and tattoos to the crafting of private and collective rituals, emic historical and theological narratives, autonomist organizational and political imperatives, the engagement with particular congregations (or not), and the conversations with other saints and spiritual beliefs, all bestow a personality on the saint and the Santa Muerte–devotee relationships. Taken together, they conform a vibrant space for bottom-up devotional agency, ownership, and intimacy.

While the symbolic, iconographic, and devotional mutations in the Santa Muerte cult have been remarkable in recent decades, they are rooted in Mexico's historically rich tapestry of Catholic, indigenous, African, and Spiritualist belief systems.

In addition, they are informed by regional social conditions as well as by multiple religious and political leaderships that resist institutionalized centralization. Shared liturgical, ritual, and theological frameworks have consolidated, but lived Santa Muerte devotion primarily features pragmatism and plasticity, dialogue, and permeability. Unlike members of other, more inward-looking new religious movements, which tend to police the boundaries with the outside world, Santa Muerte devotees have always cultivated practices of articulation and syncretism rendering 'an open cult' (Perrée 2016: 207), or what Juárez Huet et al. (2022) have called 'hinge religiosity' (*religiosidad bisagra*). In their altars and religious universe, devotees place Santa Muerte at the centre, yet often embedded in or in conversation with other religious systems – Roman Catholicism in the first place, but also Santería, and, in some congregations, other world religions. The Santa Muerte cult's disposition to appropriate, absorb, or even devour other (non-)canonical saints and religious meanings and images has been typified as 'cannibalistic' and as 'semiotic voracity' (Flores Martos 2019; Michalik 2011).[35] The cult's offline and online circulation adds more symbolic richness and opportunities to blend or articulate with other religious icons and systems.

All this has facilitated the cult's remarkable vitality, innovation, and grassroots agency: it opened spaces for devotional creativity and experimentation with private altars, public shrines and rituals, and at the level of the community as a whole. Exercising their 'religious rights', devotees continuously rewrite their beliefs and practices to give meaning to their daily challenges and anxieties (Bravo Lara 2013: 20). Section 5 showed that the trend of articulation, renewal, and expansion was met by one of curtailment and pushback, notably by the Roman Catholic Church, adverse media accounts, and hostile government policies. So far, these efforts have not been very effective. This became clear again during the 2024 federal election campaigns, when conservative political interests attempted to politicize a meme that associated an alleged image of Santa Muerte with incumbent president López Obrador and his political party. Standing in front of a massive canvas with the meme and emulating an act of exorcism, one right-wing senator pulled out a rosary and shouted, 'Stop the Devil!' Spokesmen of the Catholic hierarchy jumped on the bandwagon.[36] However, the bid to inject religious sentiments into an already polarized political environment failed. The episode demonstrated, if anything, the ignorance of political elites and religious orthodoxy concerning the lived religion of ordinary

---

[35] It also works the other way around: Santa Muerte is incorporated into Western esotericism and occultism (Hedenborg-White & Gregorius 2017).
[36] *Animal Político*, 25 April 2024, https://animalpolitico.com/politica/morena-santa-muerte-polemica.

Figure 9 Santa Muerte statue at tourist stall, Mexico City. Photo by author.

Mexicans, and its relationship to their political preferences. Presidential candidate Sheinbaum of the incumbent part won a landslide victory.

While the cult's trend of articulation and innovation has heavily outweighed that of pushback, I end by noting a tentative but discernable third trend that I call 'religious emptying' (Figure 9). In February 2023, when strolling about the beautiful Santo Domingo square in the heart of Mexico City, I spotted a small stall crammed with cheap tourist knick-knacks. Amid a multicoloured pile of bracelets, earrings, shawls, Aztec calendar replicas, and wooden toys sat a bone-coloured seated Santa Muerte statuette. By its context it suffered the loss of religious meaning, becoming just another souvenir of 'mortuary things Mexican'. Does this mean that, beyond generating devotional and iconographic vibrancy, dialogue and permeable semiotic boundaries may also prompt the mainstreaming and commercialization of the cult's key figure, and the loss of its religious meanings? When asked, the girl attending the tourist stall responded that she had no idea what the statue was about. Will further commodification compromise Santa Muerte's religious and cultural vitality? Perhaps, but in view of the cult's recent history and ample and robust popular base, the emergence of parallel circuits seems more likely – one in which Santa Muerte souvenirs are peddled, and another in which devotees continue to engage faithfully, intimately, and creatively with the saint in search of protection, order, and justice.

It is only a thirty-minute walk from the Santo Domingo square to doña Queta Romero's shrine in Alfarería street, where the outing of Santa Muerte devotion occurred in 2001. However, the historical trajectory of the Santa Muerte cult within a quarter of a century – from concealed devotion to a large, visible, and dynamic new religious movement and to the sale of the cult's central icon at tourist stalls – is socially and culturally extremely meaningful. It commands continued scholarly attention. But it should, above all, be recognized as the outcome of the faith, commitment, and investments of variegated and vigorous Santa Muerte congregations, their devotees and leaders in Mexico and elsewhere.

References

Alba Vega, C. & M. Braig. (2022). *Las voces del centro histórico. La lucha por el espacio en la Ciudad de México*. Mexico City: El Colegio de México.

Ambrosio, J. (2003). *La Santa Muerte. Biografía y culto. Veintiséis rituales personales para conseguir salud, dinero y amor*. Mexico City: Editorial Planeta.

Anonymous (2005a). El manto protectora de la Santa Muerte. *Devoción a la Santa Muerte*, 27, 22.

Anonymous (2005b). Altar del señor Jesús Padilla Alonso en la colonia Morelos. *Devoción a la Santa Muerte*, 30, 18–19.

Anonymous (2007a). *Altares, Ofrendas, Oraciones y Rituales a la Santa Muerte*. Mexico City: Ediciones Viman.

Anonymous (2007b). *El libro de la Santa Muerte: Rituales, oraciones y ofrendas*. Mexico City: Editorial Época.

Argyriadis, K. (2014). Católicos, apostólicos y no-satánicos: Representaciones contemporáneas en México y construcciones locales (Veracruz) del culto a la Santa Muerte. *Cultura y Religión*, 8(1), 191–218.

Aridjis, H. (2003). *La Santa Muerte: Sextet del amor, las mujeres, los perros y la muerte*. Mexico City: Alfaguara.

Beckford, J. (2008). *Social Theory and Religion*. Cambridge: Cambridge University Press.

Beekers, D. & P. Tamimi Arab. (2016). Dreams of an iconic mosque: Spatial and temporal entanglements of a converted church in Amsterdam. *Material Religion*, 12(2), 137–64.

Bello, J. M. (n.d.). Iglesia Santa, Católica, Apostólica, Tradicional MEX–USA. Historia y compendio de doctrinas. Unpublished manuscript.

Bigliardi, S. (2015/2016). *Si muere el Hijo de la Santa Muerte*. The symbolic codification of *Comandante Pantera*'s death at the Temple in Tultitlán (Mexico). *Studi Tanatologici-Thanatalogical Studies-Études Thanatologiques*, 8, 70–91.

Bigliardi, S. (2016). *La Santa Muerte* and her interventions in human affairs: A theological discussion. *Sophia. International Journal of Philosophy and Traditions*, 55(3), 303–23.

Blancarte, R. J. (2005). Religiosidad, creencias e Iglesias en la época de la transición democrática. In I. Bizberg & L. Meyer (eds.), *Una historia contemporánea de México. Tomo 2: Actores* (pp. 225–304). Mexico City: Oceano.

Bolaños, J. (1983 [1792]). *La Portentosa Vida de la Muerte*. Tlahuapan: INBA/Premià.

Bolaños Gordillo, L. (2015). El culto a la Santa Muerte en Tuxtla Gutiérrez: de la clandestinidad a la participación colectiva. www.chiapasparalelo.com/opinion/2015/10/el-culto-a-la-santa-muerte-en-tuxtla-gutierrez-de-la-clandestinidad-a-la-participacion-colectiva.

Bowden, C. (2006). Exodus: Coyotes, pollos, and the promised van. *Mother Jones*, 31, 5. www.motherjones.com/politics/2006/09/exodus-border-crossers-forge-new-america/, accessed 28 February 2024.

Brandes, S. (2006). *Skulls to the Living, Bread to the Dead: The Day of the Dead in Mexico and beyond*. Oxford and Malden: Blackwell.

Bravo Lara, B. (2013). Bajo tu manto nos acogemos: Devotos a la Santa Muerte en la Zona Metropolitana de Guadalajara. *Nueva Antropología*, 26(79), 11–28.

Calvo-Quirós, W. A. (2022). *Undocumented Saints: The Politics of Migrating Devotions*. New York: Oxford University Press.

Casal Sáenz, H. (2016). *La Santa Muerte: El culto de los que oran y los que matan*. Mexico City: L. D. Books.

Castells Ballarín, P. (2008). La Santa Muerte y la cultura de los derechos humanos. *LiminaR. Estudios Sociales y Humanísticos*, 6(1), 13–25.

Cervantes, A. (2011). Santa Muerte: Threatening the U.S. Homeland. Unpublished Master Thesis. Quantico, VA: Marine Corps University.

Chesnut, R. A. (2012). *Devoted to Death: Santa Muerte, the Skeleton Saint*. New York: Oxford University Press.

Comaroff, J. & J. L. Comaroff. (eds.) (2001). *Millennial Capitalism and the Culture of Neoliberalism*. Durham: Duke University Press.

Conferencia del Episcopado Mexicano (2013, October 28). Aclaraciones sobre el culto a la 'santa muerte'. www.notidiocesis.com.

De la Fuente Hernández, S. (2013). La construcción social del culto a La Santa Muerte. Estudio etnográfico en la colonia Ajusco. Unpublished Master Thesis. Mexico City: UNAM.

De la Fuente Hernández, S. G. (2015). La Santa Muerte en la vida cotidiana de una familia de la colonia Ajusco. *Vita Brevis*, 4(6), 67–78.

De la Fuente Hernández, S. G. (2016). Entre niñas blancas en la colonia Ajusco: Mirada etnográfica del culto a la santa muerte en el sur de la Ciudad de México. In A. Hernández Hernández (ed.), *La Santa Muerte. Espacios, cultos y devociones* (pp. 167–89). Tijuana/San Luis Potosí: El Colegio de la Frontera Norte/El Colegio de San Luis.

De León, J. (2015). *The Land of Open Graves: Living and Dying on the Migrant Trail*. Berkeley: University of California Press.

De León, J. (2024). *Soldiers and Kings: Survival and Hope in the World of Human Smuggling*. New York: Viking.

Del Bornio, A. (2008). *La Santa Muerte: Altares, oraciones y rituales*, with Prologue by Mons. David Romo Guillén. Mexico City: Skiros.

Denegri, L. (1978). *Desde la cárcel de mujeres*. Mexico City: Fleischer Editora.

ENCREER (2016). *Encuesta Nacional sobre Creencias y Prácticas Religiosas en México. Informe de Resultados*. Mexico City: ENCREER/RIFREM.

Flores Martos, J. A. (2007). La Santísima Muerte en Veracruz, México: Vidas descarnadas y prácticas encarnadas. In J. Flores Martos & L. Abad González (eds.), *Etnografías de la muerte y las culturas en América Latina* (pp. 273–304). Cuenca: Universidad Castilla-La Mancha.

Flores Martos, J. M. (2019). Dances of death in Latin America: Holy, adopted, and patrimonialized dead. In W. G. Pansters (ed.), *La Santa Muerte in Mexico: History, Devotion & Society* (pp. 84–110). Albuquerque: University of New Mexico Press.

Fragoso, P. (2007a). La muerte santificada. La fe desde la vulnerabilidad: Devoción y culto a la Santa Muerte en la Ciudad de México. Unpublished Master Thesis. Mexico City: CIESAS.

Fragoso, P. (2007b). La muerte santificada: El culto a la Santa Muerte en la ciudad de México. *Revista de El Colegio de San Luis*, 9(26–27), 9–37.

Gallardo, E. (2022). *Así nació el diablo: Evolución criminal de un pistolero chilango*. Mexico City: Grijalbo.

Gamboa Partida, E. (2010). El Tatuaje de la Santa Muerte en el Barrio de Tepito de la Ciudad de México. Acción e intervención en el espacio público mediante procesos plásticos contemporáneos. Unpublished Master Thesis. Mexico City: UNAM.

Garcés Marrero, R. (2019). La Santa Muerte en la Ciudad de México: Devoción, vida cotidiana y espacio público. *Revista Cultura & Religión*, 13(2), 103–21.

Garcés Marrero, R. (2020). La institucionalización del culto de la Santa Muerte: El caso de la Iglesia Católica Tradicional (ICT). *Revista de El Colegio de San Luis*, X, 21, 5–27.

Garcés Marrero, R. (2021). 'Muerte querida de mi corazón … ' La articulación del culto a la Santa Muerte con otras espiritualidades: Estudio en el Valle de México. Unpublished PhD Thesis. Mexico City: Universidad Iberoamericana.

García Astorga, B. F. (2016). Ceremonias y curación de la Santa Muerte en relación con la medicina tradicional. *Tradiciones de Guatemala*, 85, 259–82.

García Reyes, K. (2021). *Morir es un alivio*. Mexico City: Planeta.

García Zavala, R. (2007). El culto a la santa Muerte: Mito y ritual en la ciudad de México. In P. Escalante & C. Cuéllar (eds.), *Conurbados e imaginarios urbanos*. Vol. 2: Nuevas Investigaciones Antropológicas ENAH-UAM (pp. 183–223). Mexico City: INAH.

Gervasi, F. (2018). *Formas de discriminación en contra de la devoción hacia la Santa Muerte en México, en las interacciones cara a cara y en el tratamiento de la prensa digital*. San Gimignano: CISRECO Edizione.

Gil Olmos, J. (2010). *La Santa Muerte: La virgen de los olvidados*. Mexico City: Delbolsillo.

Goldman, F. (2014). *The Interior Circuit: A Mexico City Chronicle*. New York: Grove Press.

González Velázquez, E., E. García-Villeda, & T. D. Knepper. (2019). The culto of Santa Muerte: Migration, marginalization, and medicalization. In T. D. Knepper, L. Bregman, & M. Gottschalk (eds.), *Death and Dying: An Exercise in Comparative Philosophy of Religion* (pp. 63–76). Cham: Springer.

Graf, C. (2023). Devotion in the making: An ethnography of the veneration of La Santa Muerte in Los Angeles. Unpublished PhD Thesis. Leipzig: Universität Leipzig.

Graziano, F. (2007). *Cultures of Devotion: Folk Saints of Spanish America*. New York: Oxford University Press.

Graziano, F. (2016). *Miraculous Images and Votive Offerings in Mexico*. Albuquerque: University of New Mexico Press.

Gruzinski, S. (1990). Indian confraternities, brotherhoods and mayordomías in Central New Spain: A list of questions for the historian and the anthropologist. In A. Ouweneel & S. Miller (eds.), *The Indian Community of Colonial Mexico* (pp. 205–23). Amsterdam: CEDLA.

Gutiérrez Portillo, A. A. (2015). Etnografía del culto a la Santa Muerte. *Quehacer Científico en Chiapas*, 10(2), 80–90.

Hedenborg-White, M. & F. Gregorius. (2017). The Scythe and the Pentagram: Santa Muerte from Folk Catholicism to Occultism. *Religions*, 8(1), 1–14. https://doi.org/10.3390/rel8010001.

Hernández Hernández, A. (2011). Devoción a la Santa Muerte y San Judas Tadeo en Tepito y anexas. *El Cotidiano*, 169, 39–50.

Hernandez, V. (2013). The country where exorcisms are on the rise. *BBC News Magazine*. www.bbc.co.uk/news/magazine-25032305.

Higuera Bonfil, A. (2015a). Fiestas en honor a la Santa Muerte en el Caribe mexicano. *LiminaR. Estudios Sociales y Humanísticos*, 13(2), 96–109.

Higuera Bonfil, A. (2015b). La Santa Muerte en Chetumal: La expansión de un culto popular. *Caleidoscopio*, 32, 155–84.

Higuera Bonfil, A. (2016). La religión trasterrada: El culto a la Santa Muerte en Nueva York. In A. Hernández Hernández (ed.), *La Santa Muerte: Espacios, cultos y devociones* (pp. 229–50). Tijuana/San Luis Potosí: El Colegio de la Frontera Norte/El Colegio de San Luis.

Higuera Bonfil, A. (2018). La parca en mi casa: Altares domésticos a la Santa Muerte. In M. Jiménez Márquez & V. Cantero Flores (eds.), *Sostenibilidad y desarrollo humano: Una reflexión desde las ciencias sociales y las humanidades* (pp. 403–41). Cancún: Universidad del Caribe.

Higuera Bonfil, A. (2020). Evolución iconográfica de la Santa Muerte: Una historia posible. *Revista Debates Antropológicos*, 4, 127–43.

Higuera Bonfil, A. (2022). Santa Muerte Internacional: Institucionalizar una devoción. In I. G. Fierro Reyes (ed.), *México, tierra de misiones. Pasado y presente de las dinámicas espirituales* (pp. 259–96). Chihuahua: Editorial UPNECH.

Huffschmid, A. (2019). La Santa Muerte as urban staging: Notes on the images and visibility of a transgressive performance. In W. G. Pansters (ed.), *La Santa Muerte in Mexico: History, Devotion & Society* (pp. 111–35). Albuquerque: University of New Mexico Press.

Hughes, J. S. (2016). Contemporary popular catholicism in Latin America. In V. Garrard-Burnett, P. Freston, & S. C. Dove (eds.), *The Cambridge History of Religions in Latin America* (pp. 480–90). Cambridge: Cambridge University Press.

Hughes, J. S. (2021). *The Church of the Dead: The Epidemic of 1576 and the Birth of Christianity in the Americas*. New York: New York University Press.

INEGI (2021). Censo de Población y Vivienda 2020. Mexico City: INEGI.

Jiménez, A. F. (2019). Culto a la Santa Muerte: Expresión cultural y organización social en el Este de Los Angeles. Unpublished PhD Thesis. Tijuana: El Colegio de la Frontera Norte.

Juárez Huet, N., R. De la Torre, & C. Gutiérrez Zúñiga. (2022). Religiosidad bisagra: Articulaciones de la religiosidad vivida con la dimensión colectiva en México. *Revista de Estudios Sociales*, 82, 119–36.

Kelly, I. (1965). *Folk Practices in North Mexico: Birth Customs, Folk Medicine, and Spiritualism in the Laguna Zone*. Austin: University of Texas Press.

Kertzer, D. I. (1988). *Ritual, Politics & Power*. New Haven, CT: Yale University Press.

Kingsbury, K. (2021a). Death disrespected: The trials and tribulations of Santa Muerte Internacional and the martyrdom of Comandante Pantera. *Small Wars Journal*, 26 September, https://smallwarsjournal.com/index.php/jrnl/art/death-disrespected-trials-and-tribulations-santa-muerte-internacional-and-martyrdom, accessed 7 January 2024.

Kingsbury, K. (2021b). Doctor death and coronavirus: Supplicating Santa Muerte for holy healing. *Antropologica*, 63(1), 1–23.

Kingsbury, K. & Chesnut, A. (2020). Not just a narcosaint: Santa Muerte as matron saint of the mexican drug war. *International Journal of Latin American Religions*, 4, 25–47.

Knight, A. (2008). Superstition in Mexico: From colonial church to secular state. *Past and Present*, Supplement 3, 229–70.

Knott, K., V. Krech, & B. Meyer. (2016). Iconic religion in urban space. *Material Religion*, 12(2), 123–36.

Konove, A. (2018). *Black Market Capital: Urban Politics and the Shadow Economy in Mexico City*. Berkeley, CA: University of California Press.

Kristensen, R. A. (2011). *Postponing Death: Saints and Security in Mexico City*. Copenhagen: University of Copenhagen, Ph.D Series no. 68.

Kristensen, R. A. (2015). La Santa Muerte in Mexico City: The cult and its ambiguities. *Journal of Latin American Studies*, 47(3), 543–66.

Kristensen, R. A. (2016). How did death become a saint in Mexico? *Ethnos: Journal of Anthropology*, 81(3), 402–24.

Kristensen, R. A. (2019). Moving in and moving out: On exchange and family in the cult of La Santa Muerte. In W. G. Pansters (ed.), *La Santa Muerte in Mexico: History, Devotion & Society* (pp. 136–57). Albuquerque: University of New Mexico Press.

Lamrani, M. (2022). The ultimate intimacy: Death and Mexico, an anthropological relation in images. *American Ethnologist*, 49(2), 204–20.

Leija Parra, R. A. (2010). El Culto a la Santa Muerte en la capital de San Luis Potosí: Causas de su práctica. Unpublished Bachelor Thesis. San Luis Potosí: Universidad Autónoma de San Luis Potosí.

Lewis, O. (1961). *The Children of Sánchez: Autobiography of a Mexican Family*. New York: Random House.

Lomnitz, C. (2005). *Death and the Idea of Mexico*. New York: Zone Books.

Lomnitz, C. (2019). Afterword: Interpreting La Santa Muerte. In W. G. Pansters (ed.), *La Santa Muerte in Mexico: History, Devotion & Society* (pp. 183–91). Albuquerque: University of New Mexico Press.

Lorusso, F. (2013). *Santa Muerte: Patronata dell'umanità*. Viterbo: Stampa Alternativa.

Loya, J. (2009, March 24). Militares derrumben altares de Santa Muerte en Nuevo Laredo. *El Universal*.

Malvido, E. (2005). Crónicas de la Buena Muerte a la Santa Muerte. *Arqueología Mexicana*, XIII, 76, 20–7.

Mancini, S. (2012). Sobrevivir con la Muerte: Ecología de una práctica 'pagana' en el valle de México. *Artelogie*, 2. https://doi.org/10.4000/artelogie.7648, accessed 6 June 2023.

Mancini, S. (2015). Couturières de *Santos*: Personnification mythique et manipulation rituelle des images sacrées à México D.F.: la cas du *Niño Dios* et de la *Santa Muerte*. *Nuevo Mundo, Mundos Nuevos* (online). https://doi.org/10.4000/nuevomundo.68490, accessed, 28 May 2023.

Marín, C. (2007). *El hijo de la Santa Muerte: Comandante Pantera, 'una vida sin límites'*. Mexico City: Santa Muerte Internacional.

Martín, D. (2014). *Borderlands Saints: Secular Sanctity in Chicano/a and Mexican Culture*. New Brunswick: Rutgers University Press.

Matos Moctezuma, E. (2010). *La muerte entre los Mexicas: Historia*. Mexico City: Tusquets.

Matos Moctezuma, E. (2022). *Muerte a filo de obsidiana: Los Nahuas frente a la muerte*, 4th ed. Mexico City: Fondo de Cultura Económica.

McNearney, A. (2015, November 1). The death worshipping cult of Santa Muerte. www.thedailybeast.com/articles/2015/11/01/the-death-worshipping-cult-of-santa-muerte.html.

Michalik, P. G. (2011). Death with a bonus pack: New Age spirituality, folk catholicism, and the cult of Santa Muerte. *Archives de Sciences Sociales des Religions*, 153, 159–82.

Müller, S. (2021). *La Santa Muerte-Leben mit den Tod: Eine Soziologie der Verehrung*. Bielefeld: Transcript.

Navarrete, C. (1982). *San Pascualito Rey y el culto a la muerte en Chiapas*. Mexico City: UNAM.

Navarro, M. (2002). Against *marianismo*. In R. Montoya, L. J. Frazier, & J. Hurtig (eds.), *Gender's Place: Feminist Anthropologies of Latin America* (pp. 257–72). New York: Palgrave Macmillan.

Olavarrieta Marenco, M. (1977). *Magia en los Tuxtlas, Veracruz*. Mexico City: INI.

Oleszkiewicz-Peralba, M. (2015). *Fierce Feminine Divinities of Eurasia and Latin America*. New York: Palgrave Macmillan.

Pansters, W. (2015). 'We had to pay to live!': Competing sovereignties in violent Mexico. *Conflict and Society: Advances in Research*, 1, 144–64.

Pansters, W. G. (2018). Drug trafficking, the informal order, and caciques: Reflections on the crime-governance nexus in Mexico. *Global Crime*, 3–4, 315–38.

Pansters, W. G. (2019). La Santa Muerte: History, devotion, and societal context. In W. G. Pansters (ed.), *La Santa Muerte in Mexico: History, Devotion & Society* (pp. 1–57). Albuquerque: University of New Mexico Press.

Pansters, W. G. & M. Serrano. (2023). Civil-military relations in Mexico: From one-party dominance to post-transitional insecurity. *Alternatives: Global,*

Local, Political, first published online, https://doi.org/10.1177/03043 754231193895.

Pansters, W. G., B. Smith, & P. Watt. (2018). *Beyond the Drug War in Mexico: Human Rights, the Public Sphere and Justice.* London: Routledge.

Papenfuss, M. (2023). Santería in Catemaco, Mexico: Hybrid (re)configurations of relgious meanings and practice. *Interdisciplinary Journal for Religion and Transformation in Contemporary Society*, 9, 375–94.

Payá, V. (2006). *Vida y Muerte en la Cárcel: Estudio Sobre la Situación Institucional de los Prisioneros.* Mexico City: UNAM.

Perdigón Castañeda, J. K. (2008). *La Santa Muerte: Protectora de los Hombres.* Mexico City: INAH.

Perdigón Castañeda, J. K. (2015). La indumentaria para La Santa Muerte. *Cuicuilco*, 22(64), 43–62.

Perdigón Castañeda, J. K. & B. Robles Aguirre. (2019). Devotion that goes skin deep: Tattoos of La Santa Muerte. In W. G. Pansters (ed.), *La Santa Muerte in Mexico: History, Devotion & Society* (pp. 158–82). Albuquerque: University of New Mexico Press.

Pérez Salazar, G. & F. Gervasi. (2014). Santa Flaquita líbranos de los trolls. El sentido de pertenencia en expresiones identitarias en torno al culto a la Santa Muerte en Facebook. *Religioni e Società*, XXIX, 79, 84–102.

Pérez Salazar, G. & F. Gervasi. (2015). Conflicto y religiosidad en línea: Enfrentamientos en usuarios de Facebook, en torno al culto de la Santa Muerte. In R. Winocur Iparraguirre & J. A. Sánchez Martínez (eds.), *Redes Sociodigitales en México* (pp. 136–63). Mexico City: Fondo de Cultura Económica/Conaculta.

Perrée, C. (2014). Mexico, de San Judas à la Santa Muerte: Logiques votives et rituels transversaux en milieu urbain. *L'Homme*, 211, 17–39.

Perrée, C. (2016). La iconografía de la Santa Muerte: Antropología de una imagen abierta. In A. Hernández Hernández (ed.), *La Santa Muerte. Espacios, Cultos y Devociones* (pp. 207–27). Tijuana/San Luis Potosí: El Colegio de la Frontera Norte/El Colegio de San Luis.

Pescador, J. J. (2009). *Crossing Borders with Santo Niño de Atocha.* Albuquerque: University of New Mexico Press.

Pope Francis. (2016). Speech to Mexican bishops, 13 February. www.romereports.com/2016/02/13/full-text-of-the-pope-francis-speech-at-mexican-bishops.

Proceso. (2011). Detienen a David Romo, líder del culto a 'La Santa Muerte'. *Proceso*, 4 January, www.proceso.com.mx/nacional/2011/1/4/detienen-david-romo-lider-del-culto-la-santa-muerte-82324.html, accessed, 27 December 2023.

Quiroga, D. (2011). Enriqueta Romero, guardiana de la muerte. *Maguaré*, 25(1), 279–98.

Ramírez, D. (2009). Religion in Mexico, 1945–2010. In S. J. Stein (ed.), *The Cambridge History of Religions in America.* Volume III: *1945 to the Present* (pp. 57–81). Cambridge: Cambridge University Press.

Ramos, F. L. (2016). Saint, shrines, and festival days in colonial Spanish America. In V. Garrard-Burnett, P. Freston, & S. C. Dove (eds.), *The Cambridge History of Religions in Latin America* (pp. 143–59). Cambridge: Cambridge University Press.

Reich, P. (2007). Recent research on the legal history of modern Mexico. *Mexican Studies/Estudios Mexicanos*, 23(1), 181–93.

Reyes Ruiz, C. (2010). *La Santa Muerte. Historia, realidad y mito de la Niña Blanca. Retratos urbanos de la fe*. Mexico City: Editorial Porrúa.

Rodríguez López, A. (2022). San Pascualito: Etnografía histórica de las configuraciones religiosas de un santo esqueleto en Chiapas y Guatemala. Unpublished PhD Thesis. Mexico City: UNAM.

Roush, L. (2014). Santa Muerte, protection and *desamparo:* A view from a Mexico City altar. *Latin American Research Review*, 49, Special Issue, 129–48.

Rubin, J., D. Smilde, & B. Junge. (2014). Lived religion and lived citizenship in Latin America's zones of crisis. *Latin American Research Review*, 49, Special issue, 7–26.

Serna Arnaiz, M. (2017). *La portentosa vida de la Muerte*, de fray Joaquín Bolaños: un texto apocalíptico y milenerista. *Revista de Indias*, LXXVII, 269, 115–36.

Smith, B. T. (2019). Saints and demons: Putting La Santa Muerte in historical perspective. In W. G. Pansters (ed.), *La Santa Muerte in Mexico. History, Devotion & Society* (pp. 58–83). Albuquerque: University of New Mexico Press.

Smith, S. A. (2008). Introduction. *Past and Present*, 199, Issue supplement 3, The Religion of Fools? Superstition Past and Present, 7–55.

Taylor, W. B. (1996). *Magistrates of the Sacred: Priests and Parishioners in Eighteenth-Century Mexico*. Stanford, CA: Stanford University Press.

Taylor, W. B. (2010). *Shrines and Miraculous Images: Religious Life in Mexico before the Reforma*. Albuquerque: University of New Mexico Press.

Thompson, J. (1998). Santísima Muerte: On the origin and development of a Mexican occult image. *Journal of the Southwest*, 40(4), 405–36.

Toor, F. (1947). *A Treasury of Mexican Folkways*. New York: Crown.

Torres Ramos, G. (2017). El culto a la Santa Muerte: Religiosidad 2.0. *Batey: Revista Cubana de Antropología Social*, 10, 36–55.

Torres Ramos, G. (2018). Espacios para los muertos en México: Confluencia de tradiciones, culturas y creencias múltiples. *Paisagens Híbridas*, 1(1), 70–89.

Valadez, M. (2005a). El Altar a la Santa Muerte. *Devoción a la Santa Muerte*, 24, 2–7.

Valadez, M. (2005b). Rituales con yerbas. *Devoción a la Santa Muerte*, 25, 6–11.

Valadez, M. (2006). Rituales con yerbas y la Santa Muerte. *Devoción a la Santa Muerte*, 39, 6–9.

Valverde Montaño, J. (2018). La Congregación Nacional de la Santa Muerte (CNSM) como un sistema religioso del catolicismo mexicano. Unpublished Master Thesis. Mexico City: INAH.

Valverde Montaño, J. (2020). Diecisiete años de la Congregación Nacional de la Santa Muerte en Ecatepec, Estado de México. *Cuicuilco. Revista de Ciencias Antropológicas*, 77, 131–57.

Vanderwood, P. (2004). *Juan Soldado. Rapist, Murderer, Martyr, Saint*. Durham, NC: Duke University Press.

Vargas González, A. (2004). Oh Muerte Sagrada, reliquia de Dios! La Santa Muerte: Religiosidad popular en la libera de Pátzcuaro. *La Palabra y el Hombre*, 130, 101–22.

Vatican declares Mexican death saint blasphemous. (2013). *BBC News*, 9 May. www.bbc.com/news/world-latin-america-22462181.

Velázquez, O. (2005). *El libro de la Santa Muerte*. Mexico City: Editores Mexicanos Unidos.

Villamil Uriarte, R. & J. Cisneros. (2011). De la Niña Blanca y la Flaquita, a la Santa Muerte (Hacia la inversión del mundo religioso). *El Cotidiano*, 169, 29–38.

Wollen, P. (1989). Introduction. In J. Rothenstein (ed.), *Posada: Messenger of Mortality* (pp. 14–23). Amsterdam: Van Gennep.

Yllescas Illescas, J. A. (2013). La Santa Muerte hoy: Imagen personificada, dones e iniciación en el culto. *Vita Brevis*, 2(3), 69–82.

Yllescas Illescas, J. A. (2016). La Santa Muerte, ¿Un culto en consolidación? In A. Hernández Hernández (ed.), *La Santa Muerte. Espacios, cultos y devociones* (pp. 65–84). Tijuana/San Luis Potosí: El Colegio de la Frontera Norte/El Colegio de San Luis.

Yllescas Illescas, J. A. (2018). *Ver, oír y callar: Creer en la Santa Muerte durante el encierro*. Mexico City: UNAM.

Yllescas Illescas, J. A. (2023). Religiosidad cotidiana en contextos urbanos: Estudio comparativo entre el culto a la Santa Muerte de México y San Lamuerte de Argentina. Unpublished PhD Thesis. Mexico City: UNAM.

Zarazúa Campa, J. (2011). *La Santa Muerte, el mal de ojo y otras supersticiones*, 3rd ed. Mexico City: Apóstoles de la Palabra.

Acknowledgements

In researching and writing this Element I became indebted to many people, especially to the many Santa Muerte devotees and leaders across Mexico, who were invariably kind and generous in sharing with me their life stories and religious beliefs. I have learned much from the discussions and conversations with numerous colleagues in Mexico and elsewhere, especially Katia Perdigón, Regnar Kristensen, and Adrián Yllescas. The latter also proved supportive in (literally) finding my way in the Mexico City Santa Muerte community, as did my colleagues and friends Mauricio López Alvarado (in Guadalajara), Inocencio Noyola (in San Luis Potosí), Jorge Balderas (in Ciudad Juárez), Janet Valverde (in Ecatepec), and Guadalupe Palacios (in Puebla). During the last part of the writing process, I greatly benefited from the comments and suggestions of my dear emeriti Utrecht University colleagues Gerdien Steenbeek and Geert Mommersteeg, both commendable representatives of the anthropological métier. Finally, I would like to thank the series editor Rebecca Moore for inviting me to write this Element and for her unwavering support and valuable recommendations about the manuscript.

Cambridge Elements

New Religious Movements

Founding Editor
†James R. Lewis
Wuhan University

The late James R. Lewis was a Professor of Philosophy at Wuhan University, China. He was the author or co-author of 128 articles and reference book entries, and editor or co-editor of 50 books. He was also the general editor for the *Alternative Spirituality and Religion Review* and served as the associate editor for the *Journal of Religion and Violence*. His prolific publications include *The Cambridge Companion to Religion and Terrorism* (Cambridge University Press 2017) and *Falun Gong: Spiritual Warfare and Martyrdom* (Cambridge University Press 2018).

Series Editor
Rebecca Moore
San Diego State University

Rebecca Moore is Emerita Professor of Religious Studies at San Diego State University. She has written and edited numerous books and articles on Peoples Temple and the Jonestown tragedy. Publications include *Beyond Brainwashing: Perspectives on Cultic Violence* (Cambridge University Press 2018) and *Peoples Temple and Jonestown in the Twenty-First Century* (Cambridge University Press 2022). She is reviews editor for *Nova Religio*, the quarterly journal on new and emergent religions published by the University of Pennsylvania Press.

About the Series

Elements in New Religious Movements go beyond cult stereotypes and popular prejudices to present new religions and their adherents in a scholarly and engaging manner. Case studies of individual groups, such as Transcendental Meditation and Scientology, provide in-depth consideration of some of the most well known, and controversial, groups. Thematic examinations of women, children, science, technology, and other topics focus on specific issues unique to these groups. Historical analyses locate new religions in specific religious, social, political, and cultural contexts. These examinations demonstrate why some groups exist in tension with the wider society and why others live peaceably in the mainstream. The series highlights the differences, as well as the similarities, within this great variety of religious expressions. To discuss contributing to this series please contact Professor Moore.

Cambridge Elements

New Religious Movements

Elements in the Series

The New Age Movement
Margrethe Løøv

Black Hebrew Israelites
Michael T. Miller

Anticultism in France: Scientology, Religious Freedom, and the Future of New and Minority Religions
Donald A. Westbrook

The Production of Entheogenic Communities in the United States
Brad Stoddard

Managing Religion and Religious Changes in Iran: A Socio-Legal Analysis
Sajjad Adeliyan Tous and James T. Richardson

Children in New Religious Movements
Sanja Nilsson

The Sacred Force of Star Wars Jedi
William Sims Bainbridge

Mormonism
Matthew Bowman

Jehovah's Witnesses
Jolene Chu and Ollimatti Peltonen

Wearing Their Faith: New Religious Movements, Dress, and Fashion in America
Lynn S. Neal

J. Krishnamurti: Self-Inquiry, Awakening, and Transformation
Constance A. Jones

Santa Muerte Devotion: Vulnerability, Protection, Intimacy
Wil G. Pansters

A full series listing is available at: www.cambridge.org/ENRM

For EU product safety concerns, contact us at Calle de José Abascal, 56–1°,
28003 Madrid, Spain or eugpsr@cambridge.org.

www.ingramcontent.com/pod-product-compliance
Lightning Source LLC
LaVergne TN
LVHW020350260326
834688LV00045B/1644